C000302639

Ivan Little was born and bred in the heart of east Belfast, attending Belmont, Strandtown and Grosvenor High School. After training as a journalist, he worked for the *Portadown Times* and the *Belfast Telegraph* before going into broadcasting with Downtown Radio. During nearly twenty-five years with Ulster Television he has covered major stories both here and abroad as well as reporting on a regular basis for Independent Television News. Ivan is equally well-known as an actor, winning acclaim and awards for his performances in highly successful amateur and professional theatre productions, including the hugely popular *The History of the Troubles (accordin' to my Da)*. As a fanatical sports and music enthusiast, he has also written for the *Sunday Mirror* and *Ireland's Saturday Night*, and has been a contributor to the *Melody Maker* music paper.

LITTLE BY LITTLE

LITTLE BY LITTLE

IVAN LITTLE

THE BREHON PRESS
BELFAST

First published 2005 by The Brehon Press Ltd
1A Bryson Street, Belfast BT5 4ES,
Northern Ireland

© 2005 Ivan Little

All rights reserved. No part of this publication may be
reproduced or utilised in any form or by any means digital,
electronic or mechanical including photography, filming,
video recording, photocopying, or by any information
storage and retrieval system or shall not, by way of trade or
otherwise, be lent, resold or otherwise circulated in any
form of binding or cover other than that in which it is
published without prior permission in writing from the
publisher.

ISBN 0 9544867 9 X

Design: December Publications
Printed by J H Haynes & Company Ltd

For my father Billy, who passed away in June 1992,
and my mother Iola, who died in October 1993.

He did not know he could not fly, so he did.
From *The Cape* by Guy Clark, 1995.

CONTENTS

ACKNOWLEDGEMENTS

A Little acknowledgement is a dangerous thing. Leaving people out, I fear, is probably more hazardous than putting them in. So, if I am guilty of the sin of omission, my apologies go to those folk I have forgotten to include here.

First of all I would like to say a heartfelt "cheers" to Brendan Anderson and Damian Keenan at the Brehon Press for their encouragement, support and patience. The idea for this book started with what I thought was a funny aside at the launch of another of their publications by the redoubtable Paddy Reynolds. I was covering the event in the John Hewitt bar for UTV and joked with a fellow guest that my memoirs were in the pipeline. But the joke was definitely on me a few days later when Brendan rang to ask me if I *would* consider putting my experiences in journalism and acting over the last thirty-odd years down on paper.

To my partner Siofra, I must say thanks for putting up with me over the six months in which it took me to get my thoughts together and into print. Siofra also commissioned the magnificent Anto Brennan of Open Window Productions in Donegall Street, Belfast to make a model of me to accompany the political chess set she bought me for a rather significant birthday a few years back. Thanks to Anto for allowing me to include the piece in the book.

To my mucker, Albert Kirk, full-time UTV cameraman and part-time magician, I extend my sincere appreciation for his help in guiding me through the technological jungle and jargon of the computer world as I invested in a new system to compile the book. Thanks to his mum, Minnie, for the home-made soup, supplies of which sustained me through many long hours hunched over the keyboard.

To my daughter Emma: thanks for reading my manuscripts and making suggestions about what to put in and what to leave out, and thanks to her boyfriend, Kevin Lawless, for helping to solve a few technical difficulties along the way, as did my UTV colleague Alan Mackie.

Members of my family helped enormously filling in the blanks in my memory. Thanks to my nephew Jonathan's fiancée, Aislinn Coyle, for coming up with the title for the book within minutes of hearing about the project over Christmas lunch last year. I had been agonising over a suitable name for weeks. To my ex-wife and friend Joan, thanks for her input into the book and for finding newspaper cuttings from my print journalism days, which were gathering dust in her attic.

I would also like to thank the playwright Martin Lynch for contributing the foreword to the book, and cheers to him, Conor Grimes and Alan McKee, as well as Karl Wallace for the wonderful rollercoaster ride and life-changing experience that was *The History of the Troubles (accordin' to my Da)* over the past couple of years.

I would like to record my eternal gratitude to my mentor in Grosvenor High School, Mr Sam Ross, for recognising in the spotty teenager that I was something that I never even suspected was lurking in me – namely a love of the stage.

In the drama world, for their backing and encouragement, I would also like to thank Joan McCready, Walter Ievers, Ron Culbert, George Smyth, Sammy Mackie, Pat Ferguson, Kathleen Arthurs, Roy Heayberd, Peter Quigley, Paddy Jenkins, John Linehan, John McBlain, Roma Tomelty, Colin Carnegie, the late great Sean Hollywood, and especially Paddy Ormonde, one of the most inspiring directors it has been my privilege to know.

Donning my reporter's hat, and starting at the start, I would like to acknowledge the role of my first boss, David Armstrong, the editor of the *Portadown Times* newspaper. But for him, I would never have become a journalist and probably would never had had a haircut either. Along the way in journalism, I would like to acknowledge the friendship and/or help from fellow practitioners and colleagues, such as Victor Gordon, Eric Villiers, the late Harold Ford, the late Billy McCullough, the late Norman Jenkinson, Martin Lindsay, Deric Henderson, Don McAleer, Neil Johnston, Malcolm Brodie, Bill Clark, David Sloan, Maurice Hawkins, Eamonn Mallie, Billy Kennedy, Gary Honeyford, Colm McWilliams, Michael Beattie, Hugh Owens, Pat Devine, Joe Lyttle, Stephen McCoubrey, Donovan Ross, Brian Waddell, the late Derek Murray, and the late Dr Brum Henderson. To my current bosses at UTV, including Rob Morrison and John McCann, my appreciation for their backing and their trust.

I have dedicated this book to the memory of my beloved parents, Iola and Billy, but I would also like to remember someone else who is no longer with us. And that is the superlative ITN reporter, Terry Lloyd, who was tragically killed in the waste that is the war in Iraq by the wasters that are the American forces, who cold-bloodedly shot him. Terry was not only a fine journalist but a good friend and a magnificent companion also.

Others I would like to thank are the Rev Harold Good, formerly of Knock Methodist Church, Dr John Kyle, Dr Nial O'Reilly and his wife Dorothy, the late Maeve O'Reilly, Norman and Mabel Beattie, Walter Macauley, Karen Scott, John Baucher, Bobbie Hanvey, my editor Nicola Pierce, and the *Belfast Exposed* photographic agency.

Thanks, finally, to the thousands of people I have interviewed and encountered as a journalist. They allowed me to record and share in their pain or their joy, their sorrow or their laughter in a place that I have loved and loathed at various times in my life, but which I am still proud to call my home.

Foreword

by Martin Lynch

Ivan Little is more famous than Elvis. This is true. It's true in Northern Ireland anyway. As we travelled around during the tour of *The History of the Troubles (accordin' to my Da)*, which Ivan starred in, the man just never got peace. He would only be in the bar ten minutes and he would have people sitting beside him questioning, bantering and just generally chewing the fat. One night in Enniskillen it took him nearly two hours to tell me a three minute joke such was the volume of interruptions. On that basis, I'm sure it can be concluded he's at least as famous as Elvis in Northern Ireland.

Like most people, for years I only knew Ivan Little as a reporter on television. A very tall reporter. The acquaintance grew a bit more when I had occasion to be interviewed myself by the big fella. Then one day, I noticed there was an amateur production of the great American playwright Arthur Miller's *A View From The Bridge* at the Grand Opera House in Belfast. I was excited by this because, just by coincidence, I had been up to all hours the night before reading the script. I shot down to the Opera House and was delighted to find there were seats available.

I had no idea Ivan was in the play until he walked on. The next two hours provided me with one of the best single performances by an actor, amateur or professional, I have seen on the Ulster stage. In the lead part of Eddie Carbone, Ivan was a towering, powerful presence. He dominated the play. His Brooklyn accent was perfect, and his performance was seamlessly assured and practically faultless. And this was an amateur actor in an amateur production! I was blown away. To give you some idea of where I place Ivan's performance that night, I later saw Bernard Hill – he of *Boys from the Black Stuff* fame – perform the same part in the same play in a lavish West End production. Honestly, there was no comparison. Ivan's performance dwarfed that of "Yosser". As I left the London venue and walked along the Strand, I thought of Ivan. I wondered why he wasn't a professional actor.

In 2002 I came up with the idea of writing *The History of the Troubles (accordin' to my Da)*. I wrote a central character loosely based on my father and I wanted someone over fifty (sorry, Ivan) to play the part. We trundled over a list of names. When I suggested Ivan Little there was a silence. "He's a television reporter," was the reply. Few of the others had known of Ivan's acting career. One hundred and eighty-one performances and one hundred and fifty thousand people later, we know now it was a smart move. Ivan has been colossal in *History*. After watching the play in Dublin, film director Jim Sheridan declared to me that Ivan's performance was one of the best he had seen in the theatre for years.

While I'm here, I would like to say a few other things about Ivan, getting personal as it were. Ivan is a workaholic of endless energy. I remember during the rehearsals of *History* how he would arrive in for work in the mornings with a bundle of papers under his arm. He was supposed to be off on leave, yet he still felt compelled to keep abreast of the news. At lunchtime and any other chance he got he would be on the phone checking out stories, checking in with the office. He is a surprisingly shy man. Sometimes during rehearsals I had to prod him for his views on such and such a scene. He later told me he was just too preoccupied, wetting himself in case he made a mess of the part. I doubt that. Happily for us, he was our resident historian when disputes came up regarding the wheres and whens of a particular incident. Ivan had been there.

Another thing. Don't invite Ivan back to your house for dinner. After a few drinks he thinks he can drink every drink in your house and sing every song he's ever heard. Send him home about midnight to avoid unpleasantness with the neighbours. And another thing. He's a great storyteller. As a reporter he has covered almost the entirety of the troubles and lived to tell the tale. With a pint in his hand and the conversation flowing he'll have you horrified and doubled over in laughter all at the same time. And the very, very last thing. If you run a theatre company, a television company or a film company you should hire Ivan Little. You would be getting a highly talented actor, a dedicated professional and a bunch of troubles stories that will keep your entire cast and crew happy for weeks.

I've also been thinking about something else. On another level, Ivan is, or should be, a national treasure. As a news reporter for over twenty-five years, he is now a walking encyclopaedia on the events of the Northern Ireland troubles. In London they put their heroes and dignitaries in Madame Toussaud's waxworks so that people can pay in to see them. We should find a way of giving Ivan a title – something like "Doctor of Philosophy and News" – and putting him in residence, somewhere like the Linenhall Library. There he would stroll about the bookstands with his hands behind his back, dispensing information and wisdom to all those seeking explanations and first-hand accounts of our thirty year aberration. The problem is that, knowing Mr Restless, he would be very quickly bored to death.

Prologue

"Billy Wright needs to see you – and he needs to see you now," said the man on the other end of the telephone.

"Well, that could be a wee bit difficult," I replied. "I'm in Enniskillen, waiting to go on stage in a play."

"Right, I'll get back to you," said the caller, one of my main contacts in the Ulster Volunteer Force (UVF), the ruthless loyalist terrorist group responsible for hundreds of murders in Northern Ireland. Within minutes, he was back on the blower.

"Billy Wright will drive to Enniskillen to meet you. He says he really has to talk to you. *Now.*"

I tried to explain the situation again, insisting that I was in Fermanagh to act in a play in the local drama festival at the Ardhowen theatre. I couldn't simply ask the audience to hang on for a minute while I nipped outside to meet one of Ulster's most feared assassins.

"What about meeting him during the interval?" countered the go-between.

"Yes, that might work," I said. "But he'll have to be quick. The interval only lasts fifteen minutes."

As I pondered what Wright wanted to tell me that couldn't wait, the practicalities of the meeting were sorted out. Within ninety minutes, one of the strangest encounters in my journalistic career – and there have been quite a few of them – was taking place in the car park of the Ardhowen theatre on March 19, 1993. There was me, a senior reporter of many years standing with Ulster Television (UTV), sitting in the back of Billy Wright's car in make-up and costume, listening to this cold-blooded terrorist calmly outlining his grievances to me about how he believed the security forces were harassing him. He claimed soldiers were being offered £50 bonuses to stop him at roadblocks and to report back on his movements. He said it was happening day and night, even as he travelled around Northern Ireland to watch his favourite soccer team, Portadown FC.

Just what Wright, who police were convinced was orchestrating a loyalist murder campaign in mid-Ulster, wanted me to do about his problems took a wee while longer to emerge. As I tried to hurry him up, he said he wanted to record an interview with me for UTV as soon as possible. I told him that I would be in touch, but I now had to get back on stage for the second half of my play which, irony of ironies – given my companion and the nature of our meeting – was Neil Simon's classic American comedy, *The Odd Couple*.

After leaving Wright and two of his henchmen, including his Loyalist Volunteer Force (LVF) second-in-command, Mark "Swinger" Fulton, I dashed back across the car park and into the theatre again past somewhat bemused-looking patrons enjoying their interval drinks. I knew that none of them would have believed for a second the drama which had just been staged out-side the Ardhowen. It was certainly more intriguing than what was going on inside the theatre. This episode illustrates perfectly just how odd a coupling my own twin-track career of journalism and drama has been – with a notebook in one hand and a play script in the other.

The crossover between the two strands of my life has had other unusual episodes. One of them, ironically, happened just a few days after Billy Wright had been murdered in the Maze prison. That was when, early in January 1998, the reporter in me met with the most notorious loyalist and republican prisoners just hours before the actor in me bounced onstage to play King Crumble in a matinee performance of *Jack and the Beanstalk* in front of hundreds of screaming schoolchildren.

The Northern Ireland Office (NIO) had allowed a gaggle of reporters and photographers into the H-Blocks to talk to the inmates in advance of a meeting between top loyalists, such as Michael Stone and Johnny Adair, and the then Secretary of State Mo Mowlam, who was hoping to persuade them to back the peace process. It was a strange day, shuttling between the loyalist wings and republican wings, interviewing whoever would agree to talk to us. As time wore on in the jail, one of the prisoners shouted: "Come on lads, let's get a move on. Big Ivan has a pantomime to do this afternoon!"

In between my scenes in the pantomime, I scripted my television reports and, after the curtain came down, a taxi was waiting to whisk me round to our base at Havelock House on the Ormeau Road, where I edited my packages. No sooner had they aired than I was back in the Grand Opera House, pulling on my King Crumble gear, to return to the stage for the evening performance. It struck me how different the people in the audience were from the people in the Maze. Johnny Adair had let me film a piece of my report while seated on his bed, in front of his banners boasting about the Ulster Freedom Fighters' (UFF) murderous exploits, and Michael Stone had done an interview with me which was partly about his sex life!

I could never have imagined as the prison minibus drove us out of the Maze on that remarkable day that, four years later, I would be back behind bars – this time in Maghaberry prison, to perform in a play, and a play about the troubles at that! The show was *The History of the Troubles (accordin' to my Da)* written by former Official IRA activist Martin Lynch, and it was staged in the prison church in front of loyalist and republican inmates sitting side by side in Glasgow Rangers tops and Republic of Ireland shirts. I was able to record the event for posterity after the NIO gave the go-ahead for a UTV cameraman to accompany me into the jail on the strict condition that I didn't show any of the prisoners' faces or identify any of them by name. I stuck to the bargain, but the question that I knew every viewer would be asking was whether Maghaberry's best-known resident, Johnny Adair, had been in the audience. I sidestepped the no-name condition by reporting: "I can say that the jail's most fearsome inmate was not at the play. I am not allowed to reveal his name but A DARE say the man I am talking about was elsewhere!"

After our performances in the prison, Conor Grimes and Alan McKee (my two co-actors and the play's co-writers) and me agreed to take part in a question-and-answer session with these hardest of hard men. Few of them initially wanted to know about the inner workings or meanings of the play. The most popular question was directed at me: "Can you say *phenomenon* yet, big man?" The question was a reference to something else which has become a key part of my life. Ever since I agreed in 1997 to let UTV screen the outtake of me stumbling and stuttering over the word "phe-nomenon", nothing has quite been the same for me.

It was also at Maghaberry that I received the chilling query from a tough-looking prisoner, who smiled as he wondered if I was still living in Rossmore Avenue, at the top of the Ormeau Road in Belfast. Not the most comforting question to be asked by someone on remand for criminal activities. Luckily, I had just moved house to another part of Belfast. Incredibly, the cheeky bugger wanted to know where, but I didn't tell him.

The cast never knew exactly who inside the jail had committed what crime on the outside. It was surreal to think that some prisoners had probably been responsible for a few of the worst outrages of the troubles; and there they were laughing, as we presented them with ninety minutes of black comedy tinged with tragedy, based on those troubles. I also couldn't help thinking that I had covered those very same massacres for UTV, ITN, Downtown Radio, the *Belfast Telegraph* and the *Portadown Times*. From the Rose and Crown bar bomb in Belfast in the early 1970s to the other names that republican and loyalist terrorists have ensured will never be forgotten. Shankill, Enniskillen, Kingsmills, Loughinisland, Omagh, La Mon, Greysteel, the Ormeau Road, as well as the SAS ambushes on IRA units in places like Loughgall, Coagh and Clonoe.

I covered each and every one of these incidents and, in the following pages, I hope to recall what it was like to have observed at first-hand those milestones in Northern Ireland's recent troubled past. I will not, however, be offering any fresh analysis of these years. A veritable library of books has already been written for that particular job. My aim is to offer a more personal perspective of not only the murders and the bombings, but also the defining periods in the Ulster story. These include the hunger strikes; the shoot-to-kill controversies; the Maze jailbreak; the use of informers; the plight of the disappeared; the Drumcree stand-offs, and the stops and starts of the peace process. Not forgetting the plight of the victims' families and the survivors. There are also my experiences of international stories like the 9/11 bombings in New York and the tsunami disaster in south-east Asia.

Away from my role as a journalist, I will also recount my development from being an unpaid actor in the most successful ever amateur production in Ireland to my role as a professional actor in one of the biggest hits of the commercial theatre here. I'll relate

how someone like me, with two left feet, was handed a top honour from the Professional Footballers Assocation and wrote books
previewing Northern Ireland's exploits in two World Cup Finals.

I'll also explain how I was lucky enough to mingle with some
of the most famous people in the worlds of entertainment, politics, drama and sport. These encounters led to such experiences as
Maggie Thatcher feeling my knee and Ian Paisley nabbing my collar; Mariah Carey seeking my advice about the paparazzi in
County Kerry and Billy Connolly putting me in the movies;
George Best letting me share his bed and Bob Dylan snubbing
me; the Rev Jesse Jackson calling me "The Man" and Bruce
Springsteen patting me on the back. Furthermore, I'll tell you
how I broke a transvestite's heart in Boston and why I almost
became Gerry Adams for a day.

All of this and more will be revealed. Little by little.

CHAPTER 1

The Little Lad

The so-called troubles have undoubtedly been the scourge of Northern Ireland for the past thirty odd years and, although I've hated them with a passion, I have to concede my life would not have been the same without them. Not because they have made me millions of pounds, like some villains I know, but because they have provided the cornerstone of my journalistic career for decades. And without the troubles according to my own Da, I probably wouldn't be here to tell this tale.

If it had not been for all the bloodshed and hatred that blighted the border areas of Ireland in the 1920s, my father, William John Little, and his Protestant family would never have left their beloved County Cavan to move north to Craigantlet, on the fringes of east Belfast. If they had stayed on their farm in Blacklion – a stone's throw from County Fermanagh – my father would never have met my mother, Florence Iola Surgenor, in the bakery where she worked at the Holywood Arches, and yours truly would never have become their third son on September 29, 1951.

My father may have left Cavan but Cavan never really left him. After working in shops in Belfast and Lurgan, Dad set up his own milk business, Rosewood Dairy, which he ran on his own for years until my brothers, Norman and Raymond, and myself were old enough to help him. My younger sister, Caroline, was excused from the early morning awakening each day because of her tender years. I never minded helping out; in fact, I lapped up the milk round. I actually loved getting up at 4.30am on Saturdays and Sundays to be my father's little helper. His milk round was centred in east Belfast, close to where we lived in Connsbrook Avenue, off the Holywood Road.

My father was the archetypal quiet man, and as we travelled around the terraced houses off the Newtownards and Albertbridge Roads and the grander mansions of Belmont and Stormont, I felt we were the kings of the empty streets. I was as happy as a sand-boy and, though I found it hard not to nod off, I enjoyed watching the city come alive as I sat beside my Dad.

What I most looked forward to was stopping on the leafy Glenmachan Road to eat our packed lunch. On bleak winter mornings, it was invariably freezing but the memories of those times warm my heart. The phrase "quality time" hadn't been invented in those days, but that's just what the lunch break was for me – fifteen minutes of quality time when this quiet man would open up about his recollections of growing up in Blacklion and about his experiences of the Belfast Blitz. He had served in the ARP (Air Raid Protection) and one of his colleagues was Rinty Monaghan, who went on to become a boxing legend. The lunch break on the Rosewood run was just before we delivered milk and newspapers to the Royal Navy aircraft yard, now home to Belfast City airport. It was a contract that the big dairy firms in Belfast coveted and I never knew how my Dad managed to win it in the face of such competition.

In the afternoons, Dad delivered milk in Craigantlet to his erstwhile neighbours. My brothers and I would give the customers sparklingly original nicknames like "the barking dog lady" because she was a lady who had a dog that barked.

Anyone who saw me in Craigantlet the day my father died, in June 1992, probably thought I was barking too. A couple of hours after he passed away, I went to Craigantlet to leave a tube of Rowntree's Fruit Gums on the step of an old empty shop. Daft as it may seem this was my memorial for my Dad. Every day that I helped him, he bought me a packet of fruit gums from this shop. Never Rowntree's Fruit Pastilles. Never Smarties. Always fruit gums.

When it came to sharing out Dad's possessions after he passed away, I didn't want any of his watches or his rings. What I wanted more than anything were his old milk books. They consisted of lists of addresses with the amount of milk his customers used to receive, all in his immaculate copperplate writing. I still relish getting lost in my childhood recollections as I read them today, revisiting those mystical mornings by following the milk round route in my mind.

My mother Iola (a Welsh name) died the year after Dad and the tribute I paid her was also a bit off the wall too; or rather *on* the wall. My favourite time growing up in Connsbrook Avenue had been traipsing along with Mum to the shops at the Holywood Arches, a short distance away. For the simple soul that I was, the real high was to walk along a studded wall at the junction of Connsbrook Avenue and the Holywood Road while holding my mother's hand. On the day she died I returned to that very same wall to retrace my steps. What people made of me, a large man in his forties, striving to keep his balance while walking along the wall is neither here nor there.

Mum had nearly died years earlier, before any of us children came along. She had had pneumonia and was one of the first people in Ireland to be treated with penicillin. She volunteered to be a guinea pig and it saved her life, thank the Lord. She was one in a million, a gregarious woman who loved to talk, the polar opposite of my Dad. Nothing was too much trouble for my mother. Certainly no trouble of ours was ever too much for her.

One of my earliest horrors was getting caught short in P2 of Belmont Primary School on the Belmont Road. Our teacher insisted no one was to go anywhere without raising a hand and asking permission. One fateful day I just couldn't get her attention and realised that I was going to go, without going anywhere, if you understand me. Eventually she saw me and told me I could leave the room, which was the cue for the quickest dash of my life to the toilets. Sadly, I didn't quite make it and I went before I got there. I remember standing helpless in the cubicle, covered in you-know-what, in floods of tears and wondering what to do. About fifteen minutes later, my teacher arrived to investigate my disappearance.

She took one look at me and sent for my brother Raymond, also a pupil at Belmont. My hapless sibling was ordered to take me home, which he reluctantly did, on the bus down the Belmont Road. I was only about five but I still remember the ignominy of standing there in my shame and stench as shocked passengers looked on in disgust. Thankfully, Mum was at home. She flashed me a reassuring smile, saying, "Don't worry, we'll soon have you cleaned up", and without any fuss, she peeled off my soiled uniform and stood me in the kitchen sink, washing me from head to toe.

It wasn't too long before her magical maternal qualities were called on again. The occasion was a birthday party in our house. As we sat around eating our jelly and ice cream, the other children, who were a wee bit older than me, started to turn their eyes in, as kids do. It was a mystery to me. Then one of the other children scoffed at my inability to do what everyone else could do.

So, and how I lived to regret it, I managed to get my eyes to turn in. The only problem was that I couldn't get my left eye to turn out again. My horrified mother pleaded with me to straighten the eye, but as I hadn't a clue about how I had done it in the first place, I had no idea how to undo it. And then, inexplicably, I fell asleep.

The doctor arrived and even he couldn't wake me up. So they let me sleep until the next day, hoping that the great optician in the sky would correct the problem. However, I woke up with only one pupil visible; the other one had all but disappeared. I looked like something from a horror comic and was scared out of my wits, yet Mum calmly insisted that the problem would be fixed.

Dad may not have been a millionaire but he resolved to get me the best treatment that money could buy. Over the next decade I went privately to see – or half see – the best eye specialists in Northern Ireland, Miss Rankin and Mr McLaughlin. For years I wore a patch over powerful spectacles and looked, appropriately enough for someone with vision problems, a bloody sight.

The squint put an end to the story I had concocted for my friends. I told them that Ivan Little wasn't my only name; that I was also a child TV star called Mickey Dolenz, who would later become a member of *The Monkees*, but who, in the 1950s, was in a programme called *Circus Boy*. The kids seemed to believe me but any slight resemblance to him vanished once I donned my glasses and eye-patch. Long John Silver, maybe; Circus Boy, definitely not.

A series of operations straightened the eye, bit by bit, though it wasn't until the last corrective surgery in 1979, when I was twenty-eight, that the eye was finally judged perfect again and I was able to dispose of the spectacles, which had been a real pain in the glass! On the day I threw the specs away, Mum gave me a wee hug and joked, "I told you we would get your eye fixed...

though we didn't think it would take over twenty years."

The turn in my eye wasn't my only childhood nightmare. I also nearly killed myself in Connsbrook Avenue. I'm unsure as to whether it was honesty or dishonesty which almost proved fatal. I was about six years old and, at that time, people used to come from all parts to buy milk from our house. To ensure there was always change for the transactions Dad kept a box of money beside the front door, which was framed by thick glass panels.

One night as I headed up the stairs, the glint of silver caught my good eye. The temptation was too strong and I slyly snatched a sixpence from the box. It was a king's ransom in those days – two-and-a-half-pence these days – and I walked into the front room where I intended to deposit the cash in my piggy bank. As I was about complete the dirty deed, my mother's mantras about honesty and goodness crept into my mind and I just couldn't go through with it. I returned quickly to the hall. However, the squinted sprint is never an advisable act and, as I ran to the milk box, I tripped on a rug and flew ballet-like through the glass door, causing my head to split open and blood to gush forth like water from a tap.

How no one heard the glass breaking, I will never ever know. I trudged slowly into the living room, sobbing and crying out my apologies. Mum always maintained that the last thing I was worried about was the damage I had inflicted on myself. Our next-door neighbour, Mrs Montgomery, who knew about these things, took me to the casualty department of the Royal Victoria Hospital where the staff stitched me up. A doctor said that if I had gone through the door at a slightly different angle I would either have lost an ear or my life.

All this might make it seem that my life in Connsbrook Avenue was highly charged stuff. Actually, my childhood was pretty idyllic. We weren't rich but we were flush enough, unlike some people in our street, to be able to spend our pennies in an indoor toilet. My parents didn't leave us wanting for much. To answer the call of the Lord, they dutifully took us to the Congregational Church at the end of the avenue for our grounding in God. We lived in what would now be called a hotbed of loyalism, and whether I was naïve or just plain stupid, I didn't notice anything at all about a religious divide. Until, that is, one day in a little street called Brandon Parade, which ran off Connsbrook Avenue.

I must have been seven or eight years old and I was strolling down Brandon Parade minding my own business. A crowd of boys started to pick on another youngster whom I knew to see. They were calling him a "Fenian" this and a "Taig" that – completely foreign names to me. Within a short time a full-scale fight had erupted with the gang throwing stones at the other boy. Seeing that he was outnumbered I rushed to his aid. He ran up the side of his house for cover and I joined him. More stones were hurled in his direction, and he and I started to throw them and other missiles back. This went on for a few minutes until Nurse Watters, a friend of our family who lived nearby, came out and chased the gang away.

The old social conscience aspect clearly hadn't kicked in then because the only thing that was occupying my thoughts as I wandered home was what my mother was making for tea. But it wasn't just the tea that was waiting for me. Just short of our house, the same gang jumped out from behind a wall and launched into me with their fists and boots, calling me a "Fenian lover". They might as well have called me a Martian. Once they had finished with me I struggled home to seek the comforting arms, yet again, of my mother.

I asked her to explain the facts of strife and gradually a few things fell into place – like why the boy who had been attacked, and some other children who lived nearby, didn't go to the same school as the rest of us. They were Roman Catholics, my Mum said, adding that though we might not be the same as them, we weren't really any different. That cleared everything up for me then.

Mum had been the product of a typical Belfast Protestant family. Her father, William Surgenor, a staunch loyalist, had signed the Ulster Covenant in 1912; I've seen his signature on the internet site. He was also a high-ranking officer in the "B" Specials, the reserve force of the Royal Ulster Constabulary (RUC), and a fanatical Linfield supporter to boot. So much so that he banished one of Mum's first boyfriends from the family's Bloomfield Avenue home because he was a player with the rival Glentoran team.

Dad had briefly been in the Orange Order. After he quit, he took us every year to watch the Twelfth processions on the Lisburn Road, where he seemed to know everyone on parade. Yet there was no way either he or Mum would have ever permitted any of their children to join the organisation. It might have been all right for other people's children, but not for theirs.

Religion wasn't my most pressing problem. A much bigger one was soccer. Connsbrook Avenue was only a short distance away from the Oval, home of Glentoran FC. Indeed, the bedroom I shared with Norman and Raymond provided a perfect view of the main grandstand at the ground. Naturally enough, most of the people who lived around the Oval supported the Glens. In our house, it was a different story, thanks to the influence of my mother's by-now deceased father, and so blue was the hue. Norman, the oldest in the family, had been taken to see Linfield by our uncle, Tom Boyd, and he quickly became hooked. After a brief flirtation with Glentoran, I also became a Blueman on seeing the legendary ex-Newcastle United goal scorer Jackie Milburn in the flesh. He scored a fantastic goal from thirty yards in a win over

Glentoran at Windsor Park. For years, I wore my Linfield colours with pride, which probably wasn't the wisest course of action in east Belfast. I recall spending a lot of time on my back, trying to protect myself from Glentoran supporters eager to acquaint their shoe leather with my face.

No amount of kickings, however, could put the boot into my early love for Linfield. One of my heroes was Tommy Dickson, nicknamed "The Duke". He was probably one of the greatest players never to grace English football and he was also a witness to one of my worst ever sporting moments. His son Alan, who sadly died a few years ago, went to Strandtown Primary School, where I had gone after leaving Belmont. Alan might have been a year below me but he was years ahead of me and my mates in football skills. The school had an inter-class soccer tournament and as it progressed, my class, Room 23, had to play Alan's class, Room 19. Since they were younger than we were, we expected to win at a canter. I was the goalkeeper and looked forward to an easy day. However, just before the match kicked off, I noticed Tommy Dickson arriving to see his son in action. "The Duke" positioned himself just to the right of my goals and I could barely take my eyes off him, which was probably how Dickson junior ran riot. He knocked no fewer than four goals past me, and my dreams of Dickson senior recommending me as a Linfield star of the future evaporated into thin air on that humiliating afternoon.

CHAPTER 2

Who's Been Sleeping In Her Bed?

To become a professional footballer was just one of my goals; another aspiration had been to have a pop at being a rock and roll star. I had certainly been a fan for long enough, not so much by choice as by circumstance, it has to be said. My eye problems ensured that my ears were working overtime, listening to the radio. The eye specialists at the old ophthalmic hospital on Great Victoria Street (now a centre for alcoholics) carried out a number of operations on my eye to correct the squint. After each hospital visit I was banned from reading, writing and watching the comparatively new innovation, the television. The only bonus was that I wasn't allowed to go to school either, but that novelty soon wore off as boredom wore on. My only escape became the wireless. The ordinary daytime BBC shows were a yawn, but once I discovered Radio Luxembourg I was in my element. The station only broadcast late, so I dozed during the day and tuned my dial to 208 at night.

I even won a competition on Luxembourg. Listeners were invited to pick one of five songs that they thought would enter the singles chart the following week. I plumped for a song that no one remembers from a singer that everyone has forgotten. Emile Ford was his name and "Counting Teardrops" was his appalling claim to fame, though it sounded good at the time to my young ears. The song went into the charts the next week and a prize duly winged its way to Belfast. It was a copy of Ford's single – my first-ever record – but there was a slight obstacle to my enjoying this treasure: we didn't have a record player! The only time I got to play the record was when we went round to my Auntie Lily's house in Bloomfield Avenue. Her father had founded Brown's undertakers' business, so they had a few bob behind them and could afford luxuries like record players. Unfortunately, my Mum lent my record to one of my aunt's neighbours and I never saw, or heard, the disc again.

Given my blossoming love of pop music, it was only a matter of time before I thought I should have a go at singing myself, in the illustrious setting of the old bandstand on the promenade in Newcastle, County Down.

Every summer, my Dad drove the family in the milk-van to the resort for a week's holiday. My brothers sat with the suitcases on the open-to-the-elements back of the lorry, while my Mum and I (and later, my sister) sat in the more enclosed front cab. I wasn't the best of travellers and would soon be throwing up shortly after reaching our guesthouse. Mr and Mrs Stanley, who owned the B&B, would pack me off to bed with some hot milk. I would be right as rain in the morning, rarin' to go on with the high point of my year: seven days of sun, sea, sand and soccer in what I reckoned to be paradise on earth. Dad couldn't stay with us because the milk had to be delivered. How Mum coped alone with the four of us is beyond me. One of the week's highlights was Dad coming down to Newcastle to spend an evening with us.

Another thrill was entering the weekly talent competition at the bandstand, where the "pierrots" (a name derived from "pier entertainers") used to put on shows. My brother Raymond always played a song on the recorder, while every year I sang the same song, Lonnie Donegan's "It Takes A Worried Man". Raymond and I always made it through to the contest final, which was held on the Saturday night. However, as Dad collected us on Saturday afternoon just hours before the final, we never got to strut our stuff in the big showdown. I knew that the audience, who were the judges, had a soft spot for me because I looked so pathetic: a tiny wee lad in shorts with a huge patch over his left eye, singing away for all he was worth as he stared at the floor to avoid seeing anyone he knew. Raymond was no mug either. He would pick a Scottish tune to play on his recorder because our holidays invariably coincided with a major influx of tartan-clad tourists into Newcastle.

The "pierrots" used to feature old-time, variety-style entertainment together with up-and-coming pop groups like Tony G. Ford and the Seekers, the Vibratrones, and Tony and the Telstars. The main man for us was the hypnotist, Edwin Heath, who stayed in the same guesthouse as us, and would often put on a private show after his performance at the bandstand. He once put Raymond under his spell and we were able to banter him for months about his daft antics.

Raymond was the real charmer of our family. He was always in the middle of the action, was always surrounded by friends, and on holiday he always seemed to attract the girls. I developed a wandering eye too – *no*, not the squinty one – and must have been about eight or nine when I had my first major crush on another guest in our B&B, a girl about the same age as me. I didn't know how to approach her but it didn't stop me looking, even with just one good eye. Then, one night, I decided that I wasn't satisfied with admiring her from a distance and went in for the kill.

My Mum woke with a start in the middle of the night and discovered that one of her chicks was not in his nest. She ordered my brothers to search the guesthouse for me and the whole place went berserk. They were even thinking of calling the police, though the owners claimed it was impossible for me to get out of the locked house and onto the street. Amidst the commotion there was a scream. My brothers followed the shriek and a shocked woman opened the bedroom door to reveal yours truly snuggled up under the sheets beside the girl of my dreams, who was fast asleep. They shook me awake and frog-marched me back in shame to the bosom of my family, away from the bosom I really wanted to be near.

We Littles were starting to grow bigger and bigger. Early in the 1960s, my folks reckoned our house in Connsbrook Avenue was just too small. We had recently been joined by a little sister, Caroline, and so we swapped Connsbrook Avenue, which had been my ideal home for ten years, for number 19 Abbey Gardens in the Stormont area of Belfast. It was, I suppose, a move up in the world to a posher part of the city but I didn't much like it. Yes, it was a bigger house and an allegedly "better" area, but some of the local kids had notions about themselves and I felt they were sneering at the sight of my father's milk lorry in our driveway. Their comments might have been innocent enough but I couldn't take it, and eventually I went sobbing to my Dad. His answer was to show me the deeds to the house.

"We own this place," he said. "I bet there's not many of them wee buggers could say the same. Just you remember you're every bit as good as they are."

Leaving Connsbrook Avenue had meant me leaving the Boys Brigade and the Congregational Church. Dad returned to his roots by rejoining the Church of Ireland at Stormont. The church was St Molua's and I went along with him to keep him company, and promptly became a convert. I went twice to services on a Sunday, and I enrolled in confirmation classes and the choir. I also joined the youth club, and the members were an eclectic mix to say the least. Linda Martin, who went on to become a Eurovision winner was, by far, the best looking girl in the club. Paul Kirk, who played soccer for Linfield and Glentoran, and has in recent years managed Distillery, was also a member. Another regular was a chap I saw attending Linfield matches called Ronnie Bunting. His father, Major Ronald Bunting, was a well-known supporter of the Rev Ian Paisley and I thought Ronnie was just another Protestant pea in that particularly partisan pod. Ronnie had been an enthusiastic Blueman; I used to see him at matches, wearing his red, white and blue scarf. He was to nail his colours to a very different mast in the years ahead – the mast of republican terrorism.

One Christmas, I worked with him in the sorting office of the Post Office and I noticed a change in him. At Queen's University, where I often saw him at rock concerts, he was a committed and articulate socialist. I don't know how or why it happened but Ronnie, who had been a Civil Rights activist, joined the Official IRA and then the Irish National Liberation Army (INLA), where he became one of their top men. Later, he and a colleague, Noel Lyttle, were murdered in a clinical assassination which was claimed by the UDA but had the hallmarks of an SAS operation. It was believed that Ronnie had masterminded the murder of the top Conservative politician, Airey Neave, at Westminster and someone wanted revenge.

Years after his murder, I got to know Jimmy Brown, another INLA man.

He would meet me in Belfast bars to pass on statements from the organisation (especially at the height of feuds, which ripped the terrorist grouping apart and eventually claimed Jimmy's life too). During one chat in the old Washington Bar on Howard Street, I asked him about Bunting. I wanted to know if he was all

he was cracked up to be. Jimmy was almost gushing as he recounted how Ronnie, as chief of staff of the INLA, took the fight to the
British army. This was definitely a world away from the enemies
Ronnie used to have in his sights at Linfield matches all those
years before. One of my biggest regrets is that I never met Ronnie
in his later years. I often promised myself I would seek him
because I was curious about what made him tick, but I left it too
long. His wife Suzanne, who was seriously injured in the gun
attack that claimed his life, had also been a member of our youth
club at St Molua's.

One of our most famous associates – I don't ever remember
him as a fully paid-up member – was Gary Moore. He was the
guitarist who would go on to play with Thin Lizzy and later forge
a reputation as one of the world's finest exponents of blues music.
Gary lived in Castleview Avenue, the street opposite the Upper
Newtownards Road entrance to Stormont. He was the odd one
out around the area. We regularly played soccer in the grounds of
Stormont before the rangers chased us away, but Gary was always
more interested in exploring what he could do with his fingers
rather than with his feet. He went to Strandtown Primary School
with the rest of us but he never indulged in the lunchtime pursuit
of a leather ball. The first time I heard how well he could play the
guitar was around a Twelfth of July bonfire. The youngsters of
Abbey Gardens, Summerhill Avenue and the Cloghan estate built
a pretty pathetic looking bonfire on waste ground just across the
way from our house and, after lighting it, we sat around singing
songs.

It was only a matter of time before the boys who lived in the
area formed their own band, calling themselves The Barons. The
lead singer was Peter McClelland, whose future grandson Michael
was, until recently, a member of the hugely successful group,
Snow Patrol. Gary played lead guitar in The Barons. The resource-

ful manager, Willie Palmer, would often pay teenage girls in the audience to mob big Pete to encourage other girls to follow suit and rip the suit off his back!

Within a short time, Gary quit the group. He had been head-hunted by the inimitable Brush Shiels to play with his group, Skid Row, in Dublin. Many years later, I met up with Gary to record an interview with him for UTV. He turned down my request to conduct it in the shadow of Stormont and there also seemed to be some mystery regarding his age. His record company's PR man and his press releases appeared to have Gary down as being much younger than I reckoned him to be. Thankfully, my cameraman, Sam Christie, was able to help. He had been in the same class as Gary at Strandtown and had no doubt about what age he was. The PR man also told us on the quiet that we were to film Gary from a particular angle, which apparently was his better side.

Another transient member of St Molua's youth club was a bloke who formed an obsessional interest in beating me up. Vernon Baillie worked for the local butcher, delivering meat all around our district on his bicycle. This gave him plenty of mobility and flexibility for picking on me since there was no getting away from him – his two wheels were always faster than my two feet. I don't know why I was his favourite target, although I don't necessarily believe he needed a reason to give me a thumping. I often wished horrible things would happen to him. And they did.

The big white building at Stormont, the seat of Parliament, may have been a mad house but the area around it was tranquillity itself. It was almost exclusively Protestant with a small number of Catholic-owned shops at the bottom of Summerhill Avenue. No one ever bothered these shops. Until, that is, one summer evening.

We were well used to hearing explosions in the late 1960s and early 1970s but we expected to hear them at a distance. However, the blast we heard that Sunday evening was definitely a close one. We all hared down Summerhill to the shops where one business had been singled out for a pipe bomb attack. It didn't do much damage and the remains of the bomb's copper piping were lying about the street. We younger kids were fascinated by it all; the troubles had landed on our doorstep. We were all huddled around talking excitedly about the developments. Vernon Baillie even brought me into the conversation. Just then, an unmarked police car screeched to a halt beside us and two burly "peelers" jumped out to pull a startled Mr Baillie into their vehicle.

Years later, I heard all sorts of rumours about him becoming a paramilitary in the Red Hand Commando (RHC), an offshoot of the UVF. The next time I heard anything definite was that he had been murdered in a gun attack in Conlig, near Bangor, in County Down. Ironically, I covered the story for UTV and also reported on his funeral. It was funny how, after all those kickings, I could only pity Vernon Baillie.

But that was nothing compared to the emotions I felt when another neighbour became a completely innocent and random victim of the troubles. She was Lynne McClelland, who lived in the house directly opposite ours in Abbey Gardens and whose brother Pete had been the singer in The Barons. She was slightly older than I was but she was beautiful, and I could only worship her from afar. Every time I bumped into her on the street I became a tongue-tied mess. She always found something witty to say to me while I could only ever mumble nonsense in return. I would enviously watch from our sitting-room window when older blokes with money and cars would arrive at her house to take her out for the night.

Inevitably, Lynne got married to a successful businessman from County Down; but tragedy was to engulf them several years later. They were among the guests at the Irish Collie Club dance at the

La Mon House Hotel in Castlereagh, just outside Belfast, in
February 1978. During the festivities, the Provisional IRA left a
deadly bomb at a window. It was attached to a large quantity of
petrol and when it exploded it sent a huge fireball into the function room. Twelve people were killed and dozens were injured.
Among the most seriously hurt was Lynne.

CHAPTER 3

Little Looms Large

The Belfast of the 1960s could scarcely have been more trouble-free. My going downtown at night didn't cause my protective parents a second thought. They allowed me to go to pop concerts in the old ABC cinema, and Heaven help us, I was only twelve when I saw Cliff Richard and The Shadows live; I was on my own since no one else would go with me! My parents, however, wouldn't let me go to clubs or dances, so I would hang around outside the venues, collecting autographs from visiting pop stars like Brenda Lee, Georgie Fame, Lulu and The Nashville Teens. I usually ignored the local singers and groups, but when I saw an advertisement for Them at the Royal Ballroom in Dundonald, I decided to cycle up there with my autograph book.

Van Morrison was the lead singer of Them and their first ever single, "Don't Start Crying Now", had been reviewed just that morning by David Wigg in the *Daily Express*. I cut it out and took it with me to the Royal. The five members of the band were just unloading their instruments when I arrived. Shy though I was, I still managed to thrust my book under their noses and they read-ily gave me their autographs, with Van Morrison scribbling "vocals" after his name. As my way of saying thanks, I handed Van the article from the *Daily Express*, which was eagerly passed around the other members of the group. It was their first national newspaper review. Oh, the pride I felt because I had shown it to Them.

Two years later, Norman and Raymond went to see the group playing in a dance hall on the Isle of Man, where we were on holiday. Unfortunately, my Mum ruled that I was still too young to go, so I waited at the stage door and listened from there. After the gig was over, Morrison emerged with suitcase in hand. Again, he gave me his autograph after asking me to hold his bag. I went one better and offered to carry his case along the promenade to his hotel. Jeez, I was so excited to be walking with him. We even exchanged a few words about Belfast. It was the only time I ever spoke to him. I didn't want to meet him as a professional journalist because of his reputation with hacks. Van is on a pedestal with me and I never wanted to run the risk of him having a go at me. I did have a pee beside him in the toilets of the Riverside Theatre in Coleraine when UTV recorded a night of conversation between Morrison and playwright Martin Lynch, but I didn't say a word to him.

Morrison had gone to the secondary school next to my grammar school, Grosvenor High. He was five years older than me. The lads of Orangefield Secondary School didn't look too kindly on us because we had all passed our eleven-plus examinations to qualify for a grammar school education while they hadn't. We would often run the gauntlet of the Orangefield boys, with one particularly sarcastic bunch of older lads who regularly stood at the top of Orangefield Lane at Bloomfield, one of my routes to school. I'm told Morrison used to hang out there but I like to think he wasn't one of my tormentors.

At Grosvenor, I was the youngest pupil in our year. At Belmont, for some reason, I was moved from Primary One to

Primary Three, skipping out Primary Two. Mum thought it was because I was big for my age and they didn't realise how old I was. However, I'm sure they had birth certificates at Belmont and I certainly prefer to believe that they moved me because I showed some sort of promise. Whatever the reason, I did my eleven-plus a year early. My teacher Mr McNabb wasn't confident I would pass it, but I did and I went to Grosvenor a year before my time. This led to some embarrassing dilemmas because my physical development didn't quite equal that of my male classmates, who were all a year older than me. My high-pitched voice was much commented on by the deeper tones of my peers – blokes who also boasted of things in the showers which were, *ahem*, considerably better developed than my things. I suppose it was only natural for the others to give me a hard time, so to speak. Mercifully, it all changed after one summer when this Little lad returned to Grosvenor a much bigger lad. My voice had dropped along with other bits and pieces and I had shot up to a towering six feet and three inches. Even the biggest bullies had to look up to me.

Unfortunately, my extra height also attracted the attentions of the rugby coaches. They saw in this newly-grown colossus a potential giant for line-ups and the scrums. They had forgotten that I hated rugby. I didn't like the physicality of the front or second row where I was forced to play, and we were expected to play games on a Saturday which interfered with my soccer. The only way out, I reckoned, was for me not to exert myself in any matches. They could hardly pick a useless player, I reasoned. However, our games masters were beyond reasoning and insisted I had to play for one of the teams.

My next ploy was to wear my rugby gear over my everyday clothes and not indulge in anything which would get me dirty. That way I could race off the pitch at the end of the match, skip the showers, and whip off the rugby stuff to hightail it away to see

Linfield, resplendent in my pristine clothes underneath.

Once I was lucky enough to sprain my wrist. It kept me out of action for a world record period of time as the friendly family doctor kept writing me notes forbidding my participation in rugby. On my return, however, things went awry with my tactical planning. One Saturday, Linfield were playing an away game against Derry City at the Brandywell. I got my poor Mum to ring and say I was ill with the flu and couldn't possibly leave my sick bed to play rugby. Minutes later, I gleefully jumped on to a bus for Belfast city centre where I was meeting my mates to get the Derry train. But who did I meet on the way to the train station? Yes, my rugby team from Grosvenor. Forty-eight hours later, I was sent to see the headmaster Mr Moles.

I was back in his office a few years later when the school's first fifteen got into the semi-final of the prestigious Schools Cup. All the pupils were given the day off to attend the match but I stayed at home. However, one games master, Mr Cunningham, second-guessed me and discovered I wasn't at the game. Mr Moles warned me that expulsion was an option if I didn't toe the rugby line. It was the same Mr Moles who had to expel George Best from Grosvenor because of his love for soccer!

I thought it was curtains in fourth form when I appeared to be summoned to the head's office once again. However, it proved to be the start of a journey that was to change my life forever. I was copying Latin homework from another pupil when my form teacher, Sam Ross, stormed into the room and ordered me to follow him. I reckoned someone had touted me out and he was taking me to the headmaster. Then, at the bottom of the stairs, he turned right and not left towards the principal's office. We ended up in the assembly hall where he put a book into my hand and told me to read the part of the Third Murderer from Shakespeare's *Macbeth*.

My interest in drama at that point had been less than nil. I loved English classes, right enough, but I had never envisaged myself on stage. However, after that five-minute audition, I was cast in the role alongside Billy Dale and Trevor Bell as the other assassins. It was as much of a surprise to me as anyone else that I actually enjoyed this acting lark. Here at last was an arena where even my shyness wasn't a handicap; I could just hide out in someone else's character.

The next year, Mr Ross asked me to play the lead role in Thornton Wilder's gentle American story of everyday life, *Our Town*. I was in fifth form and Mr Ross told me I was the youngest pupil he had ever cast in a major part for a Grosvenor production. Mum said he probably thought I looked a lot older than I was. The part involved me acting as a narrator, linking the storyline together and I was never off the stage. It was a great role and a great play. One of the greatest thrills for me was seeing my Dad in the audience; he wasn't renowned for his theatrical outings, or any outings for that matter.

In lower sixth, I got another plum role in Shakespeare's *Much Ado About Nothing*, and another lead in Harold Pinter's one-act play, *The Dumb Waiter*. But the icing on my acting cake came in my last year at Grosvenor. Mr Ross told me he wanted me to play Sir Thomas More in Robert Bolt's heavyweight epic, *A Man for All Seasons*, which I was studying for "A" levels. Mr Ross said he would only produce the play if I took the role. I thought he was having a laugh but he told me I had the best ear of any actor in the school. This to me meant I was, essentially, a performing poodle, able to parrot Mr Ross from start to finish. Coincidentally, the cousin of the actor who played the More part in the movie, Paul Scofield, just happened to be my English teacher. He often lost his cool when I refused, as per usual, to join in class discussions analysing characters in the play. "But you have just acted

More. What do you think made him tick?" he would scream. I would just sit there and, like Tom the cabin boy in *Captain Pugwash*, I would say nothing. After the production, Mr Ross told me I should consider applying to drama school for the following year.

Yet another career beckoned in the much less exciting world of cricket. I had followed in my brother Norman's footsteps to become the statistician and scorer for the Grosvenor cricket side. Scoring is a little known part of cricket. It involves one hundred per cent concentration, recording everything that happens on the pitch, marking up every ball bowled and every run hit. Neatness and clear handwriting are a major plus.

In my finals years at school, I was approached to become the scorer for the Ulster schools representative side, and then for the Irish team. A number of officials advised me that scoring could develop into a full-time career with a county side in England; and I thought my big break had come when the BBC offered me radio work during Ireland's senior international games. Unfortunately, the dates clashed with my father needing me to help him out in his new Belfast shop, so I had to turn the Beeb down!

The summer before, I had also considered another job opportunity. At Grosvenor, one of my best friends was a nephew of John McKeague, a loyalist who set up the Red Hand Commando, an offshoot of the UVF. In the 60s, he ran a guesthouse in Portrush and I called to see him, hoping for a summer job. After a short chat, I thought better of the idea, which was just as well. It later transpired that McKeague was a sexual deviant who liked to prey on young boys. His mother had been killed in a loyalist petrol bombing in May 1971. Eleven years later, he was shot dead by the INLA, taking countless secrets about the shadowy world of loyalist paramilitaries and paedophile rings with him to the grave. The year after I left school, he had sounded me out about using my journalistic training to help him on his seedy *Loyalist News* publication. He had presumably heard about my studies from his nephew, who had kept in touch with me. I rejected his offer out of hand.

I had applied to drama schools in Bristol and London but the cost was completely out of my folks' league. And the thought of spending my life watching cricket as a county scorer in England didn't thrill me either. I knew I wanted to stay in Northern Ireland, especially as I had started going out with a girl I'd met at Grosvenor by the name of Joan Beattie. She was in the form below me but we were the same age. We met at a school formal on April 1, 1969 – that's right, April Fool's Day. We were together for the next fifteen years, first as a courting couple, then as an engaged couple and finally as a married couple (with a beautiful daughter, Emma, coming along in 1978), until yours truly – or not so truly – started to stray. But back in 1969 I had no idea what I was going to do with my life. Then, one day I read an advertisement in a local newspaper promoting Northern Ireland's first ever full-time journalism course.

CHAPTER 4

The Write Stuff

I have to confess that I had no more desire to be a journalist than to be a trapeze artist. I just liked the idea of a one year course in something, anything to keep me from a real job. So I applied and duly went for an interview for the journalism course at the old Belfast College of Commerce, off the Antrim Road. The first hurdle was staying awake because I had spent all night, like the rest of the world, watching the first-ever moon landing live on television. However, I didn't nod off and after sitting a brief written test I went into another room for an interview in front of a large panel who asked why I wanted to become a journalist. Ask me another, I thought, but I bluffed my way and my interviewers thanked me for coming along. I thought that was the end of that. Then, as I left the college, one of the interviewing panel was on his way out and offered me a lift into town. He told me, off the record, that I had impressed the panel and enthused that there was no better occupation in the world than a reporter's job.

I didn't have the foggiest idea who he was but a couple of days later I spotted him on a BBC current affairs programme. He was Jack Sayers, editor of the *Belfast Telegraph* and I thought, if he was backing me, I might have a good chance of getting on the course.

Sure enough, a letter soon arrived offering me a place for that September. I couldn't think of anything better to occupy my time. That first morning, I turned up in trepidation. I knew my bluffing about having an interest in journalism was about to be called. I was even more terrified when the rest of the students proved so enthusiastic and clued-up about what they were there to do. Many of them had been sponsored by newspapers paying their tuition fees while the rest of us had to struggle by on grants and hand-outs from our parents.

A few of those colleagues are now household names. There was Jim McDowell, the larger-than-life northern editor of the *Sunday World* and Martin Dillon, who I also worked with on the *Belfast Telegraph* before he became a best-selling writer. Other students included Gary Gillespie, now a colleague in UTV; Richard Lightbody, who became a producer of major travel programmes on national television; and Alan Watson, who is now a prominent PR professional in Northern Ireland.

Much to my surprise, as the lectures progressed, I discovered that I quite enjoyed the course. With teachers like the well-known socialist Andy Boyd, the redoubtable Dr John Harbinson, and our main tutor, Joan Fitzpatrick, the classes were rarely dull. There were feisty debates on the fast-emerging troubles, which were enveloping us all in 1969 and 1970. Not that I contributed a lot to the discussions. I was still my usual shy self, preferring to leave the arguments to the likes of Dillon, who was from a nationalist background, and big McDowell, who came from the loyalist tradition.

Away from our classes, most of us were eejits, especially on the football "field". Our college was on the quiet Old Cavehill Road and it lent itself perfectly to soccer matches without the intrusion of traffic. However, it was an indoor game that led to one of the funniest episodes of our year. Our law lecturer had foolishly left us on our own while he attended to some business. We immediately moved the desks and chairs for a quick kick-about. The ball ended up on the lecturer's desk, knocking over one of his books. The book fell open, and out of it popped a sheet of paper with our law examination questions on it. Our shorthand skills came in mighty handy as we jotted down the questions before returning the book to its proper place. Come the examination and the questions all came up! The results were predictably amazing; no one got less than ninety per cent, some were as high as ninety-seven per cent and even I got a distinction. The lecturer was almost in tears as he shared our stunning success with us, saying he hadn't thought any of us were paying any attention to him at all. Many years later, that same lecturer was devastated to learn the truth at a party attended by one of his former pupils!

However, I wasn't particularly interested in the exam results. I had decided that, despite my conversion to the cause of journalism, it just wasn't the career for me. So I buffed up my bluffing skills and got myself accepted for a teacher-training course at Stranmillis College where my girlfriend Joan would be going after Grosvenor. Then it turned out that I had done okay in the journalism examinations and the course organisers recommended me to the *Portadown Times* newspaper, where the editor was looking for a junior reporter. The thought of living and working in Portadown left me cold; Coleraine was my number one choice, but the *Coleraine Chronicle* dismissed a letter I had written to them months earlier with a two line "thanks but no thanks" reply. So, to keep the college right, I travelled to Portadown to meet with *Times* boss, David Armstrong, who gave me – of all things – a spelling test. He told me a number of other junior reporters weren't all that hot on the spelling front. Now, if there was one thing I could master, it was spelling and I can still see David's face as he looked up the weirdest words in a *Reader's*

Digest spelling competition for me to spell, and I got every single one right. There and then, Davy offered me the job. Without a second thought about Stranmillis, I said yes, also committing myself to living in Portadown rather than commuting to and from my home in Belfast. I walked out of the *Times* office stunned that I had taken a job I didn't want in a town I didn't want to live in. Maybe it was the £9 a week starting pay which was too good to refuse! Joan was as shocked as I was when I told her I would not be joining her at Stranmillis.

After working that summer in a canning factory in Norfolk, I turned down the chance to bum around Greece with my mates. Instead I returned to Portadown to start work. On August 26, 1970 I got my first front page lead in my first paper with a story from a leaked education report. Sharing the front page was a huge photograph of a mini-skirted singer: Gloria Hunniford, from Portadown, was promoting her new record. She and I would go on to share a studio in UTV, with her presenting a news programme and me reporting for it. Initially, in Portadown, I wrote a youth column for the *Times*. My first one featured an award-winning tractor driver and a new pop group, and from there I quickly expanded into news reporting and feature-writing. In October 1970, I produced a two-page spread on the closure of Portadown's historic railway station in Watson Street, whose last passenger was little old me.

Davy Armstrong bolstered my confidence by telling me he was happy with my progress and with my ability to come up with my own stories. However, he was not happy with my hair. I had grown it down over my shoulders after leaving school and now Davy urged me to get it cut, saying Portadown wasn't quite ready for my flowing locks. I compromised with a trim.

Someone else who might not want to be reminded about the way he looked in the 70s was a man who is not usually noted nowadays for his hippy attire. In 1970, Davy Jones, spokesman for the Orange Order at Drumcree throughout the long-running dispute over the annual Garvaghy Road parade, was the bass player in a rock band. A picture in my column from November 6, 1970 shows Davy and the lads with long hair, psychedelic shirts and, for some inexplicable reason, a horse. Davy had approached me to publicise his group called Machine. They described themselves as a progressive rock band who wanted to make it big in England. In the interview, which makes hilarious reading three decades later, Davy said the band were particularly fond of groups like Deep Purple and Black Sabbath! He also said one of their favourite venues was Carlton Street Orange Hall because "that is where we started off and because the atmosphere is just right". Sadly, for both Machine and Davy, they never did make it to the top. Drummer Leslie Binks did go on to establish a career as a major figure on the rock scene, however, playing with some influential bands, including Judas Priest – a name which might not have gone down so well in the oul Orange Hall.

The Garvaghy Road/Drumcree controversy may have given Portadown its later worldwide reputation for sectarianism, but in those days it was one of the quietest towns in Northern Ireland. It was strange for me to be working in the calm of Portadown during the week and then returning every weekend to the madness of Belfast to see Joan and my family. The worsening conflict didn't hit Portadown until much later and so I was able to cut my journalistic teeth on covering such thrilling markings as the local Junior Chamber of Commerce and Portadown Borough Council. Not forgetting the thrills of writing advertising features and captions for photographs.

On the other hand, I was incredibly lucky to have a colleague like Victor Gordon in the office. He was, and still is, one of the best reporters I have ever met and I have worked with journalists who have gone on to make it big in national newspapers, and in the BBC and ITN. Victor has stayed with the *Portadown Times* but that makes him no less a reporter. He could winkle a story out of anyone and has contacts coming out of every bit of woodwork in town. He could write a story quickly, accurately and with a superb flowing style. I certainly learned a lot from him about getting and shaping a story. We became close friends and I am pleased to say he's still a good mate thirty years on.

One of Vicky's greatest scoops came by complete chance and it still makes me weep with laughter just thinking about it. As well as the news beat, Vicky also covered sport, with his main passion being Portadown FC, who were managed for years by an irritable Scot called Gibby McKenzie. Vicky, it seemed, had all the players whispering in his ear, tipping him off about all the gossip about who wanted to leave Shamrock Park or who the manager was thinking of signing. A friend of mine, Billy Murray, used to play for Gibby and he told me how he offered cash incentives to players to tout on their colleagues if they suspected them of passing on stories to Vicky. Even now Billy still pesters me to reveal the moles' identities but my lips are sealed. In fact, the best exclusive Vicky ever got was thanks to a crossed line. He was making his usual weekly call to Gibby before we went to press to see if the boss had any news for him. Pigs flying across Portadown were a more common occurrence than McKenzie helping the *Portadown Times*. But on this day, Vicky got a crossed line when he put the call into Gibby. Of course, he should have hung up. Instead he waved me over to listen as the manager told the voice on the other end of the line that he would be very interested in signing him. By another fluke, I recognised the voice. Billy Millen was a Linfield player who was returning to Ireland after a spell abroad. Millen said he would like to play for Portadown and McKenzie told him he would be in touch. After they exchanged farewells, Vicky immediately re-rang the number and coolly told Gibby that he had received a tip-off that he was trying to sign Billy Millen. Gibby exploded with rage, peppering the air with expletives. He demanded to know how Vicky could possibly have learnt about his plans. Never for a second did it occur to him that it was all the result of a crossed line. I often wondered if, afterwards, McKenzie ever thought Vicky had bugged his phone.

McKenzie was later to add my name to his little black book of villains. He claimed that I had "tapped up" my mate, Billy Murray, for Linfield, the team he had supported as a boy. I told McKenzie he was talking rubbish. I admitted that I knew Billy was unhappy at Portadown and that, yes, I might just have mentioned his feelings to people around Windsor Park, including the manager Roy Coyle. However, I insisted I wasn't a go-between. Soon afterwards, Billy *did* join Linfield but it was nothing to do with me. Several years later, in a bizarre twist, Roy Coyle claimed that I was trying to unsettle Billy at Windsor Park, putting ideas into his head about leaving the club. Nothing could have been further from the truth and Billy played out many more successful years with Linfield. But it left a sour taste in my mouth.

Back in 1970s Portadown, we soon had more to worry about than football. On January 14, 1972 we had our first real taste of the troubles and I was one of the first to know. I had recently moved from my digs in Portadown to a flat in Aldervale, at the heart of the new city of Craigavon. On that Friday morning I was just leaving to catch my bus to work when there was an almighty explosion a few yards away. I raced downstairs to find a wrecked car with a policeman I knew from Lurgan barracks laying half in and half out of the vehicle. The IRA had attached a bomb to the underside of the car and designed the device to explode as soon as Detective Ian McManus started the engine. Luckily for him, he was stretching out his window to fix his radio aerial and that saved his life, leaving him seriously injured instead.

After the ambulance had gone with Detective McManus inside, it suddenly dawned on me that I should tell the media. Selling stories is the lifeblood of most provincial newspaper reporters, and in Portadown the editor of our rival publication, Dougie Sloan, had that little number all sewn up. No one dared to cross him but I reckoned I had the jump on him here because I knew he wouldn't hear about the bombing for a while. So I telephoned every news organisation north and south of the border to alert them. The following week, I wrote a first-hand account of the attack, describing how Ian never lost consciousness but "lay motionless while on his pale white face a questioning baffled look was constant until his colleagues arrived, armed to the teeth and sick to the stomachs".

On another occasion, I got the nod from a police contact that a newly-born baby had been abandoned in a house on Churchill Park in Portadown. Dougie Sloan was on holiday at the time and I flogged the story of "baby Churchill" to the world. I must say I enjoyed getting one over on Dougie because he was one of the old school of journalists who believed that rival newspapers should be rival newspapers. He barely spoke to the opposition and what really bugged me was that his staff appeared to be under instructions to ignore us too. This made life difficult for my opposite number on the *Portadown News*, Michael Beattie. He had started his job the same day as me and would go on to become a colleague on UTV. Thanks to his boss's edict, Michael and I had to meet in secret for an afternoon coffee or an evening pint. We had to choose places where the *News* bosses would not see us or hear about us. It was like conducting an affair.

I did the dirty on Michael in the early summer of 1972. We had been walking back to Portadown after covering a unionist meeting on the outskirts of town when we noticed around a hundred men in paramilitary uniforms marching up and down in the Edgarstown area. I knew instantly that this was a biggie. Tensions had been gradually rising in Portadown with IRA bomb attacks and sectarian clashes between Protestants and Catholics, but paramilitaries had never been seen on the streets. After Michael and I got back to our offices, we went our separate ways but once the coast was clear I doubled back to Edgarstown and tentatively approached the loyalists, looking for an exclusive interview. They eventually agreed to put up two masked spokesmen who gave me my front page lead on why the Ulster Defence Association (UDA) had come to Portadown. They claimed they were a purely defensive organisation who shunned criminality.

Within a month, the UDA showed their true colours with a series of brutal murders, including the shooting of Catholic pub owner Jack McCabe and a customer. Just weeks later, two more Catholics, Felix Hughes and Eamon McMahon, were subjected to horrific deaths before their bodies were dumped in rivers. Suddenly, a town which prided itself on being one of the most peaceful in Northern Ireland became one of the most violent. That September, Victor Smyth, an Ulster Defence Regiment (UDR) man who was a barber in premises beside the *Times* office in Thomas Street, was killed in a suspected loyalist car bombing in the centre of the town. My photographer, Norman McAllister, and I had been returning from a night out when we heard the blast. We were on the scene within a few minutes and discovered there was a body in the car that had taken the full force of the blast outside a Catholic-owned pub. Being this close to bomb explosions was becoming quite unnerving, especially as our own offices had been wrecked in a major IRA attack on Thomas Street. More and more, it was the loyalist paramilitaries who were taking a grip on Portadown; and I had a bit of a shock when I realised who one of the main players was.

R J Kerr was a regular caller to our office. He came in every Monday morning to give me a report on his football team, Edenderry Blues, for my junior soccer column. But then he began to discuss more sinister things. Along with Ivor Young, who was described in court as the UDA commander in Portadown, R J – or Roy as I knew him – furnished us with statements from the organisation. It wasn't long before Kerr was arrested, and one Monday morning, I had to attend a special court session in the local police station where Kerr and two other men were charged with arms offences. Kerr spotted me in the packed courtroom and shouted, "Here, Ivan, you didn't hear the result of the Edenderry Blues game, did you?" I pretended not to hear him though my blushes told a different story. Kerr's terrorist career was anything but a laughing matter. He was a close associate of the loyalist killer, Robin Jackson, nicknamed the "Jackal". Kerr's path and mine were to cross regularly down through the years. The last time I saw him was when he called me to record what would be his first and final television interview. He later died in a mysterious explosion on a boat.

One of Kerr's co-accused that Monday morning was Harris Boyle. He later became a major figure in the UVF and was said to be a close associate of the SAS soldier, Captain Robert Nairac.

Despite my early reservations about working in Portadown, I quite enjoyed my time there. I knew I wasn't there forever, yet I wasn't in any great rush to leave. Then I heard that the *News Letter* in Belfast were interested in giving me a job. Their news editor, Harry Robinson, was a former employee of the *Portadown Times* and kept an eye on the paper. He rang me out of the blue to invite me for a coffee and offered me a job in Belfast. My *Times* boss, Davy Armstrong, didn't think I was ready for the switch and offered me a £3 a week increase in salary as an incentive to stay.

In hindsight, I have no doubt that I was ready to work in the big smoke but I respected Davy and what he said was good enough for me. Harry returned several months later with an improved offer from the *News Letter*. The truth was that I rather fancied joining the *Belfast Telegraph* for a number of reasons, most notably its middle-of-the-road stance on politics. This might sound hypocritical, given that the *Portadown Times* was hardly cross-community, but it had taken me a while to realise just how much papers in Portadown were out of touch with their nationalist readers. They hardly bothered to cover Gaelic sports. I couldn't understand why since I knew my colleagues were open-minded and the editorials were totally opposed to bigotry and sectarianism. When I started up a weekly column about life in the new city of Craigavon, Catholics took some convincing that I would be able to put news about their church and sporting activities into the paper.

Even in Craigavon, which was supposed to herald a fresh start for integration in Northern Ireland, the old problems were beginning to rear their evil heads. I had a fierce row with Davy Armstrong when he buried my story about a family being forced to flee a housing estate because of their religion on page thirteen. Davy thought that putting the story on the front page, where I knew it belonged, would inflame the situation. The following year, he gave me his full backing for a major investigation into sectarianism in Craigavon. The story was the front page lead, with a two-page spread inside outlining the facts and figures of the growing polarisation.

Less than a month later, the spectre of terrorism landed right back on my doorstep in Aldervale. On December 12, 1972 a terrifying burst of shots rang out from just across the road in the Rathmore estate. IRA men fired at least twenty-four shots at a passing police car, slightly injuring one officer inside. The rest of the bullets hit our flats, one of them smashing a neighbour's window, just inches away from my own. My neighbour, who was a nurse, narrowly missed death. It was another too-close-for-comfort story for me. I resolved that it was now time to move out and on to Belfast.

My girlfriend's father, Norman Beattie, spotted an advertisement in the *Telegraph* for news reporters and I sent off my application. The interview wasn't entirely without its hitches. I had dressed up in my best suit – my *only* suit – for the meeting with the paper's editor Eugene Wason. As I walked down Royal Avenue, I realised it was also Rag Day, when thousands of students go crazy, hurling flour at passers-by while asking them for money for charity. I prayed for deliverance from their attentions, but a short distance from the *Telegraph* offices, I got zapped. Despite my best efforts to clean myself up, I had to face Mr Wason with my hair and suit streaked with flour. However, it didn't matter because I was offered a job that I gladly accepted. I returned to Portadown to work out my notice and had the satisfaction of witnessing our parent company, Morton Newspapers, taking over our old rivals, the *Portadown News*. This was definitely one in the eye for our erstwhile self-perceived "enemies".

One of my last stories for the *Times* concerned the local drama festival in Portadown. There was no way of knowing it then, but two of the people I wrote about were to establish themselves later as giants in the acting world. Liam Neeson won a certificate for his part in the play *Dark of the Moon* with the Slemish Players from Ballymena, while Ciaran Hinds was similarly recognised for his work with the Clarence Players in Belfast with the play *The Lion in Winter*.

CHAPTER 5

My Daily Bread

No one in the *Telegraph* ever knew this, but I had previously run away from a job there. In the late 60s my Dad bought a newspaper shop on the Cliftonville Road. He asked one of his contacts in the paper about getting me work as a van boy, delivering the *Tele* around Belfast. I was so shy and so scared that, as I approached the entrance to the delivery department opposite Unity Flats, I panicked and took to my heels. The same feelings came flooding back as I walked into the cavernous editorial department of the newspaper that first Monday morning: April 30, 1973. The very size of the place and the amount of people grafting away inside it scared the bejesus out of me. This time I knew I couldn't run away. Feeling like Gary Cooper on his long walk in the movie *High Noon* I trundled nervously on through to the news desk where news editor, Norman Jenkinson, greeted me with a laugh and a handshake. He showed me to my seat at the reporters' desks, where I waited to be assigned something – anything – to do. It was to be a long wait.

I read and re-read every paper but neither Jenks nor his deputy Jim Gray came near me for the first few days. I was shown around the operation and took my turn monitoring the radio broadcasts of the RUC, keeping tabs on bombings and shootings, which were plentiful. On the Thursday my big break came. An articulated lorry had overturned in the Knock area of Belfast and it took the emergency services three hours to free the trapped driver from the cab. I filed my story and it made the front page lead. Of course, it wasn't long before I was covering murders and bombings on an almost daily basis. I was also part of the team that covered the big court cases at the Belfast City Commission on the Crumlin Road. The stories from here were usually riveting and the craic over lunchtime pints with other reporters, like court veteran Paddy Topping, was mighty.

It was just a little bit further up the Crumlin Road on June 26, 1973 that I experienced one of the most frightening episodes of my journalistic career – a close call, which still sends shivers racing up and down my spine. On that morning, the news desk sent me to the home of Irene Andrews, a twenty-five-year-old former *Telegraph* employee, who had just been savagely murdered along with SDLP politician, Senator Paddy Wilson, on the Hightown Road outside Belfast. The couple had had their throats slashed, and were stabbed more than fifty times. I had been dispatched to the house where Irene lived with her mother to see if the family wanted to say anything about the killing. It was around 9.00am when I walked up to the front door dreading, as usual, the awful prospect of asking the bereaved about their feelings. As I knocked, a voice screamed at me from the garden next door, "Get the fuck out of there, now."

I turned to see a couple of men gesturing wildly at me. Unnerved, I quickly returned to the main road and they dragged me away from the Andrews house. After telling me they were RUC officers, they asked, "Who the fuck are you?" I showed them my press card and asked them what was going on. One of them replied, "The family didn't want us to tell Mrs Andrews about

Irene until the morning. They wanted us to let her sleep, and she's not up yet." The import of their words sank in immediately. If Mrs Andrews had answered her door in time I would have blurted out the dreadful news to her. "So why didn't you stop me sooner?" I gasped. "I could have killed the poor woman with the shock of it all." They claimed they hadn't seen me going through the gate – all six feet and three inches of me.

Two UDA men were convicted of that unspeakable slaying and I encountered both of them in my UTV years after they were released from jail. In January 1988, David Payne was charged with possessing hundreds of guns that had been smuggled into Northern Ireland from South Africa by loyalist terrorists. As he was led into court in Craigavon, Payne looked over at the packed press benches and shouted, "Oh aye, there's Ivan Little and the rest of the shit."

Payne's co-accused, John White, later became a prominent spokesman for the UDA-linked Ulster Democratic Party and a close ally of "Mad Dog" Johnny Adair. White frequently set up shows of strength for Adair and his fellow gangsters and, after one particularly vicious feud within the organisation in February 2003, a ruthless UDA godfather, John Gregg, who was once jailed for shooting Gerry Adams, was murdered by Adair's faction. Media reports said White had gone to ground after Gregg's killing but he rang me to deny he was hiding from anyone and that he would record an interview with me if I came to the Shankill estate which had been his and Adair's power base. Naturally, I pressed White about the Gregg murder and finally he admitted to being indifferent about it. Within hours of the broadcast hundreds of UDA men invaded the lower Shankill to drive Adair's supporters out of their homes, including John White and Adair's wife Gina.

It was so different from twelve months earlier when the UDA were engaged in another bloody feud with the UVF. On that occasion, White arranged to do an interview with me at the entrance to the Lower Shankill estate. He was accompanied by David Payne, the first time I had seen him since he hurled abuse at me in that Craigavon court. As I interviewed White, dozens of UDA men ran past us. Soon I could hear the sound of breaking glass: rampaging gangs were attacking UVF homes, including that of the organisation's mentor, Gusty Spence. When my cameraman and I set off to investigate, we were threatened by the UDA, leaving us in no doubt as to what would happen if we filmed them.

Threats from the UDA weren't particularly new: I had received a few since joining the *Belfast Telegraph*. By 1974 I had become a point of contact for the terrorists when they wanted to claim responsibility for this killing or that bombing. One day, the man on the other end of the telephone, who called himself Captain Black, read out a statement threatening to kill *Telegraph* journalists if the newspaper didn't change what he called the "pro-Republican stance" in their leader columns. He added that the killings would begin with Ivan Little and another reporter. I asked the man why we had been chosen, and with typical loyalist logic, he replied that our names had been on the front page of the paper that day. I tried to explain that this was insane since neither of us had anything to do with the editorial policy of the paper. Furthermore, I told him, the UDA had a nerve phoning me to publicise their statements one day and telling me they were going to kill me the next. Without betraying any appreciation at the ridiculousness of his next words, he said, "Calm down now Ivan, there's nothing personal in this." So there I was – the recipient of the world's first non-personal death threat, not knowing whether to laugh or cry. Within minutes, my *Telegraph* colleague, Wendy Austin, now the voice of the BBC's *Good Morning Ulster* programme, nipped next door to McGlade's pub and got me a very large brandy. In consultation with the paper's bosses it was agreed that I would stay on in my job; only a few months earlier, a colleague had been relocated back to Britain after the IRA had warned him off. I just couldn't envisage the UDA backing up their ludicrous threats with real actions.

Of course, they weren't the only loyalists unleashing terror and torture in the 1970s. For years, the UVF's "Shankill Butchers" sparked fear right across Belfast, under the leadership of that vicious, cold-blooded psychopath, Lenny Murphy. They slaughtered the softest of soft targets.

One of their killings, in particular, left me numb. I had met Stephen McCann on September 8, 1973 when I covered a twenty-four hour vigil outside Belfast City Hall organised by the group, "Witness For Peace". Its founder was the Rev Joseph Parker. His fourteen year old son, also called Stephen, was one of nine people killed by the IRA when they exploded twenty bombs in just over an hour on Bloody Friday, July 21, 1972.

At the vigil, I noticed the seventeen-year-old Stephen McCann standing alone in his St Patrick's secondary school uniform and thought he was one of the youngest peace campaigners I had ever seen, so I decided to interview him about why he was there. I recorded his words in the *Telegraph*: "Like thousands of others, I am fed up with violence. I feel it is my duty to identify with peace. This is my first peace vigil." It wasn't his last and he even wrote a song entitled "What price peace?" which was sung at rallies. It was just three years later when Stephen became a victim of the violence he so despised. As he walked his girlfriend home in October 1976 the Shankill butchers grabbed him and dragged him into a car. They shot him dead in the Glencairn estate and then they slit his throat.

I frequently thought of Stephen as I stood at the City Hall, waiting for a taxi or a lift after a drunken night out in those

Telegraph days. There weren't many pubs opening late at night. Still my mates from the reporting staff – Deric Henderson, Don McAleer and me – always managed to find a watering hole, like McGlades, the Blackthorn or the Wellington Park hotel on the Malone Road on a Friday night.

My daytime pursuits were varied. Sometimes it was a plethora of pints in McGlades, the favourite watering hole of local and visiting hacks; other times it was a secret visit to dodgy strip-clubs in Hill Street or North Street; or else – hand on heart, this is true – it was a trip to a bingo hall to pass away more innocent lunch-hours. How my poor mother and my fiancée Joan stuck it, I don't know. I blame the *Telegraph* for opening a social club *on* the premises. Talk about all our birthdays coming together! It was, quite simply, too much of a temptation: to be able to nip upstairs after work and sink a pint or two was a godsend. Not that we were violent or loutish when lagered: we were just a wee bit lippy.

On one particularly memorable night, I tried to act as a peacemaker after a number of people abused another *Telegraph* employee from the marketing department. Their target then, without justification, rounded on me and so I got stuck in to him too. It resulted in a ban from the social club along with a warning from the editor, Roy Lilley, about how to behave in the future. The poet laureate of the *Telegraph*, copy-taker Bob Young, was forever writing poems about the dastardly deeds of the reporting staff. This one was addressed to me, supposedly from the committee of the Social Club after another night on the tear:

> *For singing songs when you were jarred*
> *We have decided you are barred.*
> *You have caused no end of a hubbub*
> *Up in the anti-Social Club.*
> *The songs were tuneless which were sung*

Along with Henderson and Young.
When you were asked to play it low
Your answer was, "Ach, f*** off Joe."
The full committee duly met
And here's the sentences they set:
A month for Bob Young and yourself
For nearly wrecking wee Joe's health.
Another month for you and he
For singing loudly all off-key;
And furthermore another one
For joining in with Henderson.
A month's suspension for each ditty,
Thus rules the Social Club committee.
Another month for being plastered
And one for calling Joe a... bad man.
And as your crime was so abhorrent,
All sentences won't run concurrent.
We hope in future you'll be wary,
Signed Donaghy, the Secretary.

My own behaviour did improve in August 1974 after Joan and I got married in Knockbreda Methodist Church and moved into a flat in the Belmont area of east Belfast. When I returned from honeymoon, I was asked to take on the role of rewrite man for news stories, which meant collating information from reporters on the ground and turning that information into a snappy and understandable story. One of the rewrites that I will never forget concerned the IRA killings in September 1975 of Judge Rory Conaghan in the Malone area, and Resident Magistrate Martin McBirney in the Belmont district. I had actually passed the latter murder scene on my way to work and saw the police arriving but I didn't realise the significance of it all: an embarrassing secret I have kept to myself. Until now.

I also have to confess that I nearly missed another huge story around that time. I had been sent to Ballyhalbert to cover the funeral of Northern Ireland's legendary comedian, James Young. All was going swimmingly as I drove right behind the convoy of funeral cars en route to Belfast. At the village of Ballywalter, however, I realised something was missing – the funeral cortege. My mind had drifted away to other things and the mourners' cars were no longer in front of me. Panicked, I doubled back and asked a man standing by the road if he had seen the funeral. He said it had turned off before Ballywalter, taking a different route from the one I had expected. Thus began one of the fastest, daftest car chases imaginable as I searched for the cortege. Thank God, I managed to locate it, just before it reached Young's Group Theatre where a large crowd waited to pay their last respects. The funny man would have been highly amused, I'm sure, if he had seen my antics that day.

Around this time my contacts with the paramilitaries were increasing, although one incident still beggars belief. Two UDA men had been kidnapped at a time of tension between the UDA and the UVF in April 1975. Initially it was thought the IRA had abducted Hugh McVeigh and David Douglas, and the UDA told me they would kidnap a Catholic a day until their men were freed. However, it soon became obvious that this was really the work of the UVF. A spokesman for that group repeatedly insisted to me that they weren't responsible. Then, in September 1975, the bodies of the UDA men were found in a shallow grave near Islandmagee and four UVF men were later convicted of the murders. One of them was the UVF spokesman who had time after time denied any knowledge of the victims' abduction.

The UVF couldn't really deny involvement in another barbaric massacre in 1975. I was one of three reporters assigned to the story of the Miami Showband slayings. Posing as members of the security forces, the terrorists had flagged down the musicians' bus after a gig in Banbridge. Their plan had been to hide a bomb on the minibus and the subsequent blast, the UVF thought, would convince the world that the showband had been ferrying explosives for the IRA. But the bomb went off prematurely and the UVF gunmen opened fire on the band as they stood helpless by the roadside. Three of them were killed while two members of the UVF gang were also blown to pieces by their own bomb. One of them, Harris Boyle, had appeared in court alongside Roy Kerr in Portadown when Kerr had asked me about the local football results.

Boyle was also suspected of involvement in the Dublin and Monaghan bombings, which had claimed thirty-three lives in August 1974, and which the UVF didn't actually admit responsibility for until nineteen years after the fact when I was given a statement belatedly owning up to the atrocities. The UVF said they had carried out the bombings but denied they had received any assistance from the security forces, as had been suggested in a television documentary. Everyone believed the first part of the statement; few believed the second part.

Another major story I covered in 1975, and which still fascinates me, was the meeting between Protestant church leaders and top-ranking Provisional IRA men in a hotel in Feakle, County Clare. The churchmen, including the former Methodist President the Rev Eric Gallagher and Dr Arthur Butler, a Church of Ireland Bishop, wanted to tell the IRA that they couldn't shoot and bomb Protestants into a united Ireland. In return the Provos – among them David O'Connell, Seamus Twomey and Kevin Mallon – gave the clerics a list of demands to take to the British government. By a complete fluke I made a telephone call to a man who had helped set up the meeting – I never have and never will identify him – and he couldn't have been more co-operative. I met him in east Belfast and he gave me the chapter and verse on the talks. He even predicted the Provos might call a brief ceasefire as a sign of goodwill, providing me with a story which the *Telegraph* ran as a front page lead and which, subsequently, proved to be one hundred per cent accurate.

I had the perfect handle on developments from my contact and over the following months I was able to help the *Telegraph* lead the way in the coverage of the secret liaisons between the government and the IRA through a group of intermediaries, including a number of the Feakle churchmen. I was also told by contacts in the negotiations that there was a plan to open what were called "incident centres" manned by Sinn Féin members; now, whatever happened to them? Unfortunately, the moves towards peace came to naught. The Provos were quickly back on the warpath and the loyalists, as ever, weren't far behind them.

Suddenly, my news reporting came to an end – albeit a temporary one. I was called into the editor's office and for once it wasn't a rollicking that awaited me. Roy Lilley informed me I was being promoted to the *Telegraph's* illustrious features department just days before my twenty-fourth birthday. This made me one of the youngest reporters ever to be elevated to the loftiest heights of the *Tele*. Sadly, the job proved to be as boring as Old Nick at times.

CHAPTER 6

Among The Elite

The word about my promotion in the *Telegraph* spread quickly. All the lads in the reporters' room seemed fine about it. Mind you, they were probably glad to see the back of me and looked forward to my hosting a major piss-up. But the response from one of the features department's most respected writers caught me on the hop. Alf McCreary, an award-winning hero of mine, came to me and said, "Welcome to the elite." He told me I was joining the *Telegraph*'s finest, which would result in big changes in my life. I hadn't a clue what he was talking about but I determined that if he was referring to my choice of company in the *Tele*, there was no chance of change. My drinking mates were not up for negotiation; in fact my opportunities to booze actually increased.

One of my main duties in the features department was to co-edit the *Ulster Log*, a daily diary column, with Neil Johnston who, like my old sparring partners Henderson and McAleer, came from Omagh. Nelly had also cut his journalistic teeth on the town's weekly publication, the *Tyrone Constitution*, a name that sounded more like an illness than a paper.

Neil was, and is, a gifted writer with the cleverest and gentlest turn of phrase. He enjoyed a jar, so we were well suited. What made Neil even better company was his love of Irish traditional music. I was fast turning into a fanatic, which was unusual enough for a Prod and a Linfield supporter. Even more unusual was the fact that I had been introduced to Irish music by an RUC man I was on holiday with in County Donegal. The off-duty cop had stuck a tape in his car stereo as we returned from a visit to Lackagh Bridge near Carrigart, where we were staying. I remember that moment as if it were only yesterday. The music blasting through the stereo sent a rush of excitement right through me.

"What on earth is that?" I demanded of my peeler pal. He replied, "They're a band called Planxty, and that song is called 'Cunla'."

I had to have more and he made me a copy of the tape that I listened to at every possible moment. I bought every Planxty album on the market and I went to see them in concert. I wanted to know more about Irish music, and there was no better teacher than Neil Johnston. He gave me books as well as records and told me endless stories about the history of the music, and about the great exponents of the form, including the great Arty McGlynn, his old friend from Tyrone. Arty was still playing guitar with showbands but he has since gone on, as Neil knew he would, to become one of Ireland's finest traditional players.

Neil knew his stuff and was an excellent musician too, especially on the mandolin, as he demonstrated at sessions, Christmas parties and fleadhs. He introduced me to a whole new world. Such was our shared love of the music that we started to mention it in our column at every turn, helping to promote new folk venues like the groundbreaking Sunflower Club in Corporation Street.

Away from the diary column, I was further expected to contribute weighty articles for the paper's feature pages. I couldn't understand why we were given so long to write them. It wasn't uncommon for us to be given several weeks to research and write *one* article. I remember one colleague who shall remain nameless, taking *a week* to compose the first paragraph of one feature. Writer's block, they called it. I preferred to rattle out my articles as quickly as possible to ensure there was always time for an afternoon shandy.

Working in the features department reminded me of my initial spell in Portadown. Once again, the troubles weren't high on the agenda, with the thinking behind the diary column being to provide a bit of light relief for the readers. In two years, I wrote maybe a couple of articles which were related to the real world of Northern Ireland, and I don't remember many of my colleagues writing much about the troubles either. I would write thoughtful pieces on such worthy subjects as the future of the shipyard, or local people taking part in *Mastermind* and *Opportunity Knocks* on TV, or people complaining about bans on denim in pubs and hotels… and so on, and so on.

Of course, there were features I enjoyed writing: mainly on folk and rock music, and on sport. There was the lengthy piece I wrote on whether or not there should be an all-Ireland soccer team. That was right up my street. I got weeks to research it and got to meet some of my gods in the Northern Ireland squad like George Best and Pat Jennings. Bestie kept me waiting ages in a hotel in Templepatrick but I would have waited forever as just shaking his hand was a thrill, never mind sitting on his bed for the interview. Trying to imagine what had been going on in the bed before I arrived was also intriguing. George was all for a united Ireland team and told me it was about time the authorities "got up off their arses" and did something about it. Only Jimmy Nicholl, who came from the loyalist Rathcoole estate, expressed any reservations. Well, he did have to go home, now and then.

I also went to Dublin to meet members of the Football

Association of Ireland, as well as another football hero of mine, the former Leeds United midfield general, Johnny Giles. He was, by 1977, back home in Ireland managing not only his country but also Shamrock Rovers. He was signing a procession of up-and-coming Irish and English players for the Rovers. After interviewing him at his Milltown office, I jumped on a bus back to the city centre. I was carrying my overnight bag, which obviously gave the bus conductor ideas because he sat down beside me and asked me, all conspiratorial-like, if I was one of Johnny's new boys. Sinful though it was, I told him I *was* thinking over an offer but I couldn't divulge my name because I was playing for a well-known club in the north and didn't want my transfer leaking out. He refused to take a penny off me because he was a Rovers fanatic and said he would keep an eye out for me in the park.

Another feature I loved doing was about one of my all-time comic heroes, Billy Connolly. I had first seen him in Edinburgh in 1974 before he became well known outside of Scotland. I actually thought I was going to see Billy Connolly the folk singer, unaware that he was actually a comedian. By the end of the show, I was raving about him and took a couple of his records back home where they proved a huge hit with visiting friends and relatives. Naturally when Connolly came to Belfast in 1975 I was head of the *Telegraph* queue to volunteer writing about him. He sold out his two gigs at the old ABC cinema and I was at both of them. He said he would steer clear of the troubles because "if I lived here, the last thing I would want to hear about on a night out is the troubles". Still he couldn't resist it when a girl rushed forward to hand him a rose as he walked on stage. He took a sniff of it and shouted, "BOOM!" At the start of the second show he looked around the theatre and declared, "It's great to be in Belfast. I feel like Abraham Lincoln!"

After the two shows I went to see Connolly for a formal interview, which was recorded and partly used in a documentary about Billy's Irish tour. The finished product was called *Big Banana Feet* and was shown in cinemas all over the UK. However, my movie debut was missed by most of the people who saw the film on the night I was there. As soon as they saw the curtain coming down on the concert footage they got up and left, missing me and my moment of stardom with the Big Yin.

About seven years later Connolly came into UTV for a live interview with Gloria Hunniford. Of course, I was full of the bull with my colleagues, recounting my last meeting with Billy and wondering if he would remember me. I popped downstairs to see him in the make-up room and he immediately said, "Hey, you're the big lad who interviewed me in the movie." I was most impressed because in the intervening years I had shed my glasses and grown a beard. "You honestly remember me?" I asked him incredulously. "No", he laughed. "Your mate Gary Gillespie warned me you would be plaguing me!" After we got to talking, I said that I had never received a fee for the movie, to which Billy replied, "Join the queue, pal!"

The odd Connolly moment wasn't enough to lift my depression in the *Telegraph* features department. The boredom was only offset by the demands of the diary column where Neil and I both had an eye for the absurd. The little funnies we unearthed still make me laugh even today. One of my favourite stories involved a friend of mine who lived in a tough, paramilitary-controlled area of east Belfast. I didn't identify him but I related how one night, after the boozer, he telephoned the police to tip them off about suspicious activity in his street. He had seen a group of men moving what he thought could be guns into an unoccupied house. Minutes later, someone was hammering down his front door and a squad of policemen and soldiers pushed past him to carry out a search. My mate was appalled and demanded an explanation before he remembered that he had given the cops his own name and address.

Neil and I both relished finding daft letters and quotations in the weekly newspapers. For example, there was the strike organiser who announced, "We had a hundred per cent turnout for yesterday's stoppage but today it's even better"; and the loyalist newspaper which berated the IRA for "shooting two defenceless Pakistanis from India". There was also the woman who wrote to a paper urging milkmen to close peoples' gates behind them "because the birds were pecking the tops off the bottles"; and the traditional Irish music club in Connemara which advertised itself with the slogan "No Pop Here".

We also loved uncovering people with particularly appropriate names like Mr Salmon, the winner of a Fermanagh fishing competition or Susan Brew, the winner of the 1977 Miss Harp beauty competition; the chairman of the mid-Antrim savings committee was Mr LSD Seymour, while the local bank manager was called Mr Handforth. Not forgetting Mr Porter, the Guinness publicity officer. Another gem I saw with my own eyes was in Ballycastle, where a hotel had a sign on its ground floor window advertising "Teas" while on the first floor there was a sign for "High Teas".

Working in the features department meant that I had Saturdays off and I was able to accept an invite from the *Tele*'s sports team to cover Irish League soccer matches for them. I was often sent to report on Linfield's games, which wasn't exactly a hardship. My coverage of one game was immortalised in a poem by the *Telegraph* bard, Bob Young – not because the report was good but because I had managed to miss a goal.

Let me put forward the case for the defence. The game in question was Distillery versus Glentoran. It was played at the home of junior club Brantwood at Skegoneill Avenue since Distillery were homeless at that point. The facilities for the press were dire: all we had was a tiny hut, which made it virtually impossible to see the entire pitch.

The Glens romped the game four-two, or so we thought. At one point, the legendary reporter Paddy Toner returned to the hut to tell us he had fallen into a hole and asked us who had scored the third goal for Distillery. We all reckoned it must have been the shock of the fall and ignored Paddy. Final score, then: four-two to the Glens. You can imagine my horror the next morning when I picked up the *Sunday News* to read my report and saw that the scoreline was Distillery *three* goals to Glentoran's four. My piece was complete with a description of a goal I hadn't seen. I phoned the paper and was told that one of their reporters, Stanley Wright, was at the game in his capacity as a Glentoran supporter and he had definitely seen a third goal for Distillery, so he added it to my story. Talk about embarrassment! Malcolm Brodie and his entire sports department in the *Telegraph* ribbed me about my miss for months, with Bob Young capturing it in verse:

> *Hark to the tale of Ivan Little*
> *Who's asking Malcolm for acquittal*
> *On charges brought last Saturday*
> *About the goal that got away*
> *In a League match up at Skegoneill*
> *(No date's been set for the appeal).*
> *Sez Malkie, told the goal was missed:*
> *"Ah thought he was a journalist;*
> *Ah'll nivver send him out again,*
> *Ah have to think of the ISN* [Ireland's Saturday Night].
> *Such lax reportin' ah n'er saw,*
> *Good job it didn't mean a draw.*

Ah canny be everywhere massell,
The Shrine and Skegoneill as well.
Ah've covered games from pole to pole
And can't recall a single goal
In ma career ah've ever missed
In cold sobriety or pissed."
Meanwhile, until his case is heard,
To send him out they're still prepared.
But if the ground's devoid of lights,
They'll give him telescopic sights.

Bob Young was probably the funniest man in the *Telegraph*. Every Twelfth of July he would send a story to a new reporter in the newsroom telling them that two lodges had pulled out of the Orange processions – Turf Lodge and Nazareth Lodge! One of Bob's favourite stories was about the time he took copy over the phone from Malcolm Brodie after some fabulous game somewhere in the world. Malkie started his report with the intro "Magnifico, Magnifico, Magnifico", to which the laconic Young responded, "Yes, okay, Malkie. I heard you the first time."

Another bonus about covering soccer on a Saturday was getting the chance to report on the matches for the English papers. I must have passed muster because Bill Clark, the ace writer with the *Sunday Mirror*, asked me to write his column for him whenever he was on holiday or away covering an international story for the paper. I also opened up another outlet for my work with the *Melody Maker* music weekly. I would write the occasional article on folk music or review a rock concert. Not that there were many gigs to cover in the 70s.

Writing the *Ulster Log* and features for the *Telegraph* wasn't really my cup of tea. I missed the cut and thrust of news reporting in the furnace of Northern Ireland's troubles. The money in the

Telegraph was also pretty appalling. I had started in 1973 on less than £2,000 a year and by 1977 my salary had barely doubled – and I was supposedly in one of the most prestigious jobs in Belfast journalism. I made up my mind to get out and was offered a job in Dublin with the *Irish Independent,* along with Deric Henderson. However, I got cold feet because Joan was pregnant and I didn't think the upheaval of a move to Dublin would be in anyone's best interests. Therefore I somewhat regretfully said no to the *Indo.* Deric also turned them down.

I was still unsettled and when I saw an advert for a duty news editor for the comparatively new Downtown Radio station in Newtownards, I thought I should apply for it. The wages were around £5,000 a year and I had been impressed with the station's set-up when I wrote a feature on its first morning on St Patrick's Day, 1976. There was just a slight problem: the news editor was David Sloan. He was a former colleague on the *Belfast Telegraph* and I bitterly regretted giving him a hard time at the staff Christmas party several years earlier. I was completely in the wrong and wouldn't have blamed him if he had told me to get stuffed when I rang to see about applying for the job. Fortunately he was a bigger man than that and told me to go ahead. I got the job but there was soon another complication.

Harry Robinson, who had offered me jobs on the *News Letter* before, rang to say the paper wanted me to join their news desk team. Harry invited me for a drink and told me I was a newspaper man, not a broadcaster, but I declined, telling him that I fancied the new challenge of the spoken word. I was one of five journalists who handed in their notice to the *Telegraph* on the same day. Indeed a Dublin-based magazine, *Hibernia,* even ran a story, calling us quitters and revealing that the total number of departures in 1977 alone was no fewer than twenty-five.

My first night as a duty editor at Downtown, St. Valentine's

Day 1978, was a nightmare. I had been training for several weeks but no amount of training could have prepared me for this initiation. Early in the evening, an Army helicopter crashed in South Armagh, killing all passengers, including a major. It was quickly discovered to have been an accident and not a terrorist attack. However, it was still a big story, or so I thought until just before ten o'clock that night. An ambulance man, who also worked as a freelance photographer in County Down, rang Downtown to give us a tip-off about a story. It made us forget all about the helicopter crash. Bill Hamilton said there had been a report of a massive explosion at the La Mon Country House Hotel at Castlereagh, with many casualties. Sod's law, of course, dictated that this was also the night a colleague, Harry Castles, was having a party in his Bangor home and the entire Downtown newsroom staff were planning to go.

None of the off-duty reporters really wanted to miss the festivities but Eamonn Mallie wasn't difficult to persuade. He, like me, was fairly new to the broadcasting game. Some people thought his strong South Armagh accent difficult to understand. However, in the short time I had been at Downtown, I had grown to like and respect Eamonn immensely. He was a terrier in that once he got hold of a story nothing could shake him off it. I knew Eamonn was the man for La Mon and he certainly didn't let me down. He was quickly on the scene and his first phone call chilled me to the bone. He was convinced this was a huge atrocity with the death toll running into double figures. I raced to the news booth to read out a news flash and we followed it up with regular updates, featuring Eamonn's superb on-the-spot reports. At one point, he talked of seeing what looked like logs being taken away from the inferno of La Mon, adding that he now knew them to be bodies.

His reporting was intuitive and inspired, and our bulletins left the BBC floundering in our wake. A few days later, I discovered that I had known some of the people caught up in the La Mon massacre. Among them was my old Abbey Gardens neighbour, Lynne McClelland. A number of people who died had been friends of my brother Norman and his wife Maureen.

Downtown wasn't all downbeat, though. Certainly, I missed the frontline reporting but I enjoyed organising the coverage of stories and shaping the bulletins, though we occasionally had to fly by the seat of our pants. Sometimes the early morning presenters didn't turn up on time and us humble hacks had to get the station on air. I remember one time, Eamonn Mallie and me flicking every switch in front of us while I started to read the news, both of us wondering if what I was saying was actually being heard by anyone. A quick-thinking Eamonn raced out to his car and switched on his radio before sprinting back to give me the thumbs-up that, yes, the listeners could hear me loud and clear.

Sometimes too, after late boozy nights, the early morning presenters weren't really in the mood to communicate with their public. One DJ grunted at me when I said I really thought he should at least say good morning. He shrugged his shoulders and mumbled that he just couldn't form a proper sentence. It was an hour and a half before he strung two words together on air.

The highlight of my two years with Downtown had nothing to do with the radio station at all. A few months after joining the team, my daughter Emma was born. I had been out on my usual Saturday razzle at the football and Joan and I had had a slap-up meal, thinking the birth was a long way off. Then, in the middle of the night, Joan shook me – literally and figuratively – with the words every sleepy, hung-over father-to-be dreads to hear: "I think the baby is coming." Fourteen hours later, after I had been sent packing from the delivery room by a nurse who said I was more of a hindrance than a help, Emma arrived. And it was love at first sight.

The early morning and late night shifts at Downtown suited me well, allowing me to become a part-time househusband. Since duty-editors rarely worked in the middle of the day, I could collect Emma from her childminder while Joan was at work, teaching in a local primary school. Nevertheless, there was something missing at Downtown. Although I enjoyed the responsibilities that working on the news desk brought, and I loved reading bulletins or voicing news reports, I was still office-bound. Nothing could disguise the fact that I was longing to be out on the road again.

The one thing I didn't miss during my days as a feature writer on the *Telegraph* and as a Downtown news editor were my close links with paramilitary organisations. The republicans and the loyalists went elsewhere with their statements. Until, that is, a call came through to me on December 3, 1979. I picked up the phone to hear a voice I didn't recognise telling me that I should alert the police to a body in a house on Brooke Crescent, off the Black's Road in Belfast. The caller said the UFF had murdered David White after breaking into his home. For an instant, I briefly thought about sending a reporter to the house before informing the police. Instead, I rang the RUC at the same time as one of our off-duty journalists was rushing out the door of her Belfast home. The telephone call was not a hoax. Mr White's body was found in his house.

A more pleasant phone call came my way around the same time – the call that took me to UTV, thus ending my four year exile as a real reporter. Terry Smyth, who had been on the news team at Havelock House before becoming sports editor, told me that UTV were interested in having a yarn with me. So I went to see the news editor Ian Sanderson and programme controller Brian Waddell and they offered me a staff job. After two years in

Portadown, four years at the *Telegraph* and two years in Downtown, I reckoned two years in UTV couldn't hurt.

Two decades on I am, as I write this, still there.

CHAPTER 7

The Big Picture

The private words of welcome to Ulster Television from Belfast journalism's wisest and wiliest old fox had been simple, straightforward and unexpected. Ivan McMichael prowled the courts in the mornings looking for stories and spent the afternoons in the UTV newsroom writing scripts. He said to me, "Well, big man, you can say goodbye to your privacy and to your marriage." I nearly choked on my pint as the wee man delivered his greeting in Maxies, the pub next door to Havelock House, on my first Friday night outing after work. Television was apparently a nail in the coffin of marriage for reporters and presenters. He also predicted I would miss the anonymity of papers and radio. I respected Ivan a lot but I treated his warnings with scorn. However, with the benefit of hindsight, I can now say the wee bugger was right on both counts.

In 1980, a more pressing concern for me was getting used to the very different demands of television, as opposed to radio and newspapers. Looking back from the high-tech comfort zone of today, it's almost impossible to understand how we ever got anything on air, considering we were still using film for covering the news. Nowadays, digital pictures can be on the screen within seconds of them arriving in Havelock House. In my early days, we had to get the film back to UTV and hand it to a processor to develop it in the darkroom. Then, after a forty-five minute wait, we had to go through the processed film with an editor, who cut it frame by frame, matching our timings, before sticking it all together. That roll was then played into the news programme as us reporters sat in the studio reading our scripts live on air. We had to hope against hope that the words would fit in with the pictures and pray that we would finish reading the script before the soundbites of our interviewees kicked in. Nowadays, we have the luxury of recording our reports onto a digital tape, and if we stumble or stutter, which the world knows I occasionally do, we can just re-record the words. It is wee buns compared to the old days.

I was quickly thrown into the fray at UTV. However, my first live studio report had to be abandoned after Joan rang to say she was feeling ill, just before I heard the sound of her hitting the floor. I immediately telephoned the police who called an ambulance to take her to hospital. I raced to the Ulster Hospital at Dundonald to discover she required immediate surgery. Eventually, I was told that Joan had had an ectopic pregnancy – the foetus was forming in the fallopian tube outside the womb – and she had been just ten minutes from death. I could scarcely take it all in and, after making sure Joan was okay, I returned home to look after Emma. It was only then that I realised Joan had been pregnant again and that we had lost the baby. But I didn't have long to dwell on it; within minutes of my returning Emma to her cot, she tumbled out of it onto her head and proceeded to vomit all over herself. Even for someone with my rudimentary knowledge of medical matters, this was clearly not a good sign. The doctor was called and, after he gave the all clear, I had to clean Emma from head to toe as well as changing her sheets.

When I eventually got back to work for real, the stories came thick and fast. An RUC contact tipped me off that a body found near Dunmurry in March 1980 was that of German industrialist Thomas Niedermayer. Then all hell broke loose after three members of staff of the Kincora Boys Home were jailed for sexually abusing children in their care. The case led to years of accusations that security service bigwigs, civil servants and loyalists had been involved in a paedophile ring at Kincora. This was a wee bit close to home because I used to catch my bus home from school at Kincora's front gates.

The following year was dominated by the republican hunger strike at the Maze and I seemed to spend every waking hour for months standing outside the prison as papal envoys, Irish Government officials, Red Cross teams and politicians went inside to urge Bobby Sands to end his fast. No one really imagined that the government would allow Sands to die. Pundits reckoned that the government would play their usual game of brinkmanship and then, just before anyone died, they would go part of the way towards meeting the hunger strikers' demands. The pundits had reckoned without Maggie Thatcher.

In March 1981 I had to interview her for UTV at the end of a twenty-four hour visit to Northern Ireland. We, the BBC and RTE, were told we could each have four minutes with the "Iron Lady". No more, no less. Still, as I was going in to bat first, I decided to chance my arm. I asked her about the issues of the day, with the hunger strike being the main thrust of my questioning. She vowed she wouldn't yield to the prisoners' demands. I maintained eye contact with her so that she was looking right through me with her cold, piercing stare. It was disconcerting but I persevered. I noticed her press secretary, Bernard Ingam, coming into my line of vision behind her to make it clear my time was up. However I wasn't sure if, by drawing his fingers across his throat, he was telling me to stop or if he was indicating what he planned to do to me. Eventually, I wrapped up my interview and Ingam exploded, claiming I had overrun my slot by six minutes; at which point, Mrs Thatcher leaned forward, put her hand on my knee and whispered, "You will never do that to me again, young man." I never did interview her again.

She was true to her word on the hunger strike. On May 5, 1981 Bobby Sands died, sparking violence all over Ireland. His funeral two days later was an historic moment. You didn't have to be a republican sympathiser to realise that something was changing, and that things would never be the same again. Over one hundred thousand people turned up to the funeral and it clearly wasn't just IRA supporters. The depth of feeling against the British Government, and Maggie Thatcher, hung heavy in the air.

Over the next days and months, I covered most of the hunger strikers' funerals. As the death toll grew, you sensed a mounting despair among republicans that no matter how many coffins came out of the Maze, Mrs Thatcher would not budge. Gradually, relatives of hunger strikers were ordering doctors to save their loved ones, to prevent them dying for nothing. The hunger strike was over before the year was out. On October 3, I was told to be at the UTV fax machine to receive a communiqué from the jail, a document I still have in a scrapbook. It said that the prisoners had reluctantly decided to end their fast because they had been robbed of the hunger strike as an effective protest weapon due to the campaign waged against "our distressed relatives by the Catholic hierarchy, aided and abetted by the SDLP and Free State political parties".

It was also during the hunger strike era that I made a truly bad call. I was reporting on the death of teenage west Belfast girl, Julie Livingstone, who had been killed by a plastic bullet fired by soldiers on the Stewartstown Road. It didn't take long to establish that she was an innocent victim who hadn't been involved in the disturbances following the death of hunger striker Francis Hughes. However, I completely lost the plot after an RUC contact rang me to say that Julie Livingstone was a relative of a man who had been jailed in connection with the murder of a Protestant man six years earlier. Our lunchtime news was fast approaching and I didn't take time to think things out. Unfortunately, I played up the murder angle big time, tarring the girl with the same brush as her relation. Her family was, quite rightly, furious with the report. It was an unforgivable lapse on my part, which I regret to this very day.

Something else that haunts me was the murder of Catholic, Joe Donegan, in October 1982. Mr Donegan was abducted by the UVF after leaving a club on the Falls Road. It was, they said, their response to the IRA kidnapping part-time UDR soldier, Thomas Cochrane. The Provos probably killed him immediately but they released a statement saying they were "interrogating Mr Cochrane because of his crimes against the nationalist community". This was the cue for the UVF to capture Mr Donegan. The loyalists put out a statement saying they would release him only if the IRA freed Mr Cochrane. However, the BBC and Downtown Radio refused to carry the statement after the police tried to play it down. The UVF also contacted a priest and a nationalist councillor but the statement still wasn't broadcast.

As chance would have it, I was on call for Independent Television News (ITN) that weekend. The UVF contacted me and left me in no doubt that they had kidnapped Mr Donegan. I ignored the RUC advice and ITN ran my story as their lead on the lunchtime bulletins. No sooner had the item gone out on the news than my phone started ringing. First it was the RUC demanding to know how I could be so sure of my facts – a question repeated by a procession of journalists from newspapers and broadcasting organisations. I gave them all the same reply: I was sticking by my story. I was becoming thoroughly fed up with the calls and was increasingly off-hand with the doubters. At that stage I didn't know the name of the Catholic victim and when Anne Donegan rang from the *Irish News*, I had no inkling that she wasn't calling as a journalist, but rather as Mr Donegan's daughter. I felt physically sick when I found out the identity of the man and his relationship to Anne. I have wondered long and hard if I could have done anything more to save Mr Donegan by trying to set up a process of mediation. But the reality is that Mr Donegan, like Mr Cochrane, was almost certainly killed within a short time of his abduction. The offer to release him was nothing more than a cynical ploy.

Mr Donegan's body was later found behind the house where Shankill butcher Lenny Murphy had once lived. The following month, the IRA went into the heart of the loyalist Glencairn estate to kill Murphy, and put an end to the reign of terror which I had covered throughout the 70s and 80s.

Another man who reappeared from time to time in my life in the 80s was Edward Manning Brophy. He was the man police were convinced had carried out the La Mon bombing in 1978. Brophy was arrested after the bombing by the RUC following an unprecedented number of anonymous telephone calls from people in west Belfast touting him as the bomb-maker. It was even suggested that the Provos had grassed on him because he had messed up the construction of the bomb. He was later acquitted, and I was one of the few reporters in court that day. After he walked free, I asked his lawyer if Brophy would give me an interview. The lawyer told me that his client had no way of getting home to Turf Lodge and if I gave him a lift he might answer a few questions. So I drove him home and, after being reunited with his family, he agreed to an interview where he denied he had anything to do with the La Mon bomb.

That wasn't my last contact with Brophy. In February 1988 two UDR soldiers were murdered by an IRA bomb near the Castlecourt shopping centre, which was then under construction in Royal Avenue. The bombers had gained access to the site after holding security guards captive in their homes. I got a tip-off from a police contact that one of the security guards was a certain Edward Manning Brophy. I went back to the same house in Turf Lodge. This time, he wouldn't go in front of the cameras but he vehemently denied that he had been a willing participant in the bombing. He also told me that the boss of the security firm that employed him was a unionist politician, which really put the cat among the political pigeons.

It was a difficult story to report because of the laws of libel. Brophy was guilty of nothing. However, unbeknown to me, a colleague used the old journalistic trick of giving my information to a Westminster MP, the Rev William McCrea of the Democatic Unionist Party (DUP). He used parliamentary privilege to name Brophy in the House of Commons.

This all happened just days after I had completed a special half-hour programme for UTV on the tenth anniversary of the La Mon bombing. I interviewed several survivors and many of the people who had lost relatives. The one victim I really wanted to include in the programme was Lynne McClelland, my old neighbour. By this stage, Lynne had moved to Canada to try to exorcise the ghosts of La Mon. She had received horrendous burns and needed extensive skin grafts, which were described to me by a specialist from the Ulster Hospital at Dundonald in an interview for the programme. I tried to persuade Lynne to record an interview with me in Canada but she just couldn't do it.

As for Brophy, the whispering campaign against him never diminished. The UFF later shot and seriously injured him in a gun attack at a shop in Corporation Street.

Every day in the 80s seemed to bring more and more of the same: shootings, bombings and grief. A new phrase had also entered the dictionary of death, "shoot to kill". The RUC denied they were adopting any such policy but the evidence seemed to suggest otherwise.

The first of the controversial killings was in Craigavon, less than a mile from where I had once lived. Three IRA men – Sean Burns, Eugene Toman and Gervaise McKerr – were shot dead by police, who said they had failed to stop at a roadblock. The trio were unarmed and their car was riddled with dozens of bullets. Within hours of the shooting, I was standing on the doorstep of McKerr's house with his widow, Eleanor. She wanted to do an interview, claiming her husband had been murdered, but she didn't want to admit he was in the IRA. I suppose I did overstep the mark in telling her that the dogs in the street knew McKerr was a leading Provisional and to deny it would weaken any argument she might put forward about the killings. Eventually, she said that "even if he was an IRA man, he didn't deserve to die like that". My coverage, which questioned the official version of events, was rebuked by the RUC. Journalistic colleagues, who seemed to believe everything they were told by police headquarters, were critical of my scepticism. But questions had to be answered. The police killed more unarmed men in contentious circumstances in Lurgan and Armagh over the next couple of months. Coincidence, some called it, while others reckoned it was a concerted campaign. Of course, at the same time, the Provos were still engaged in their own murderous onslaught against the security forces and their tactics weren't exactly wholesome. Being caught in the middle of a propaganda war at that time was a real dilemma for journalists. My only way to cope was to believe no one; I assumed they were all lying – the police, the army, the Provos and the Prods.

After the "shoot to kill" controversy, the authorities then came up with a new weapon in their war against the paramilitaries: the supergrass. Terrorists were offered new lives and big pay-offs to turn tout on their former colleagues. The trials were among the most dramatic events I have ever witnessed. And I covered most of them: Joe Bennett, the UVF informer; Christopher Black, the IRA supergrass; and Harry Kirkpatrick, the Irish National Liberation Army (INLA) tout were just some of them. Not forgetting Raymond Gilmour, William "Budgie" Allen, Bobby Quigley, Kevin McGrady, Stanley Smith, Patrick McGurk, William Skelly, Jimmy Crockard, and so on. The sight of dozens of the most violent men in the province sitting side by side in specially extended docks was surreal and fistfights were common occurrences. The violence normally erupted inside the courtrooms, except for the time when legal reporter Mickey Donnelly and I once, unwittingly, provoked a riot *outside* in the foyer.

It happened after a judge cleared his court of members of the public due to a fight breaking out between the prisoners and their police guards. Mickey and I sneaked out a side door to file our stories. As we compared notes on what we had seen, a relative came over to eavesdrop. When she heard the words "blood" and "batons" she ran over to dozens of other relatives and told them the RUC were giving their men a hammering. The women went crazy and tried to break down the doors. The police emerged from the courtroom and were promptly attacked by the womenfolk, with the fighting spreading right across the foyer of Crumlin Road courthouse. Mickey and I discreetly took off to the safety of the canteen to discuss what was now an even better story.

The initial entrance of informers into court was always electric. They were invariably dressed in the slickest of suits and were clearly told not to look at either the defendants baiting them from the dock, or at their own loved ones pleading with them from the public gallery not to give evidence. For some supergrasses the emotion of it all was just too much. UVF informer, Clifford McKeown, couldn't cope with the pleas from his mother in the gallery and from his brother Trevor in the dock. Yes, he had put his own brother in the frame. Among the other twenty-eight in the dock was one Billy Wright. McKeown told the judge on a Friday that he didn't want to continue with his testimony. The judge told him to think it over and come back on the Monday with a final decision. As he left the court, I recognised a carload of top UVF men from Portadown waiting for McKeown. I reckoned that might be the last we would see of him but he returned three days later to say he was withdrawing his evidence. His mother came over to me afterwards and said her son wasn't such a bad lad really. She handed me a poem he had written to her, which proved to her how good a son he was. Twenty years later I was in court to see McKeown jailed for life for a sectarian murder. His brother Trevor was similarly sentenced for another killing.

The most bizarre of all "paid perjurer" cases, as republicans called them, centred on informer Robert Lean from Belfast. The police were cock-a-hoop after his arrest and many leading IRA figures were rounded up. Gerry Adams gave me an interview in which he attempted to play down Lean's significance in the Republican movement, despite my producing a photograph of the two of them together. A few weeks later, Sinn Féin put the word out that we should attend a news conference in west Belfast, where there would be something of interest for us. Indeed there was: Robert Lean, large as life. He had escaped from his handlers at Palace Barracks in Holywood by nicking one of his minders' cars and driving himself out of the place, bold as brass. He told the news conference he was retracting his evidence and that it was the police who gave *him* the information about top republicans, not the other way around. Lean was arrested outside the news conference and most of the people he implicated were freed. It was a major blow to the supergrass system. Within years the entire tactic had crumbled after judges expressed concerns about the touts on whose word people were being convicted.

Dozens of men were freed on appeal. As they walked out of court, the men's leaders spoke to the press. Most of them are now dead. The police never apologised for recruiting informers, which they described as their most successful tactic to curb terrorism. Around thirty informers were recruited and over three hundred men were charged, taking some of the most active and dedicated terrorists off the streets for years. The number of killings and bombings fell dramatically but many people viewed the system as another form of internment. Catholic and Protestant church leaders denounced the employment of touts, including the Rev Ian Paisley. In fact, the system managed to achieve the impossible – uniting loyalists and republicans in a joint protest outside Crumlin Road courthouse in 1983. It sounds crazy, I know, but I recently rooted out the pictures again to make sure my memory wasn't playing tricks on me.

Most of the informers were never heard of again, though some did come out of the shadows to write books. I even took one supergrass back to the Shankill Road in Belfast, the very area where he had operated as a UVF killer. Jimmy Crockard gave evidence against fifteen of his erstwhile colleagues and I tracked him down to England. His cover was blown when his real identity emerged in a Gloucester court after he was charged with assault. To my surprise, Crockard agreed to be interviewed on camera and, not long afterwards, he rang to tell me he was in Belfast. He said he would have no difficulty about returning to the Shankill, with a camera crew recording his every move. A UVF contact later told me Crockard would have been a dead man if he had been spotted. "People don't forget squealers," he said.

And something the IRA won't forget happened back in 1983: the Maze jailbreak. I was on call for ITN that Sunday in September and received a tip-off from an RUC contact that something big was going down at the prison. I alerted my crew and was at the jail within twenty minutes. Unbelievably, I drove straight up to the front gate, which was wide open. A journalistic colleague had beaten me to the punch. I found Anne Cadwallader standing around, looking as bemused as me. We wondered where everyone was. We could see the open gate but there wasn't a sinner in sight. Well, not for a few minutes anyway. Suddenly, the army arrived in their Land Rovers to seal off the entire area. A family, who lived nearby, were kind enough to take me into their house and told me I could wait there until my crew arrived. But they never came. They had stopped several miles away from the jail to get pictures of the security forces driving aimlessly around the area. By the time the team tried to approach the Maze, the police and army had got their act together, setting up roadblocks to stop anyone getting through. I stayed in that house for hours, telephoning the news to ITN that no fewer than thirty-eight IRA men had escaped. I cursed my luck that that there I was, surrounded by potential interviewees to the biggest jailbreak in British history, without a camera crew to film them!

At one point, soldiers burst into the house where I was holed up. They didn't check the occupants' identities and accepted my story that I was just visiting. It was a strange way, I thought, to search for jailbreakers. For all they knew, I could have been one of the Provos' top men.

Eventually, however, I came out of hiding and returned to Belfast to file my main report for the evening news.

To this day I wonder what might have been, not only because of the missing crew situation but also because it's possible I could have been standing outside the jail as the escapees were escaping. Earlier that morning, long before the jailbreak, I took a call from the same RUC contact regarding a search for a republican prisoner who hadn't returned to the Maze from parole. I told ITN that the only way to cover it would be to get pictures of the prison and record a piece to camera at the gates. But the news editor wasn't interested. It could have been a very different story if he had been.

CHAPTER 8

From *Marita Ann* to Kegworth

I was now being asked more and more to cover the main Ulster news stories for the ITN bulletins, which were networked right across Britain. ITN's presenters, who included Sir Alastair Burnett, Sandy Gall, Martyn Lewis, Selina Scott and John Suchet, were household names to millions of television viewers. I was particularly chuffed when Sir Alastair wrote a special article for UTV's twenty-fifth anniversary magazine praising the contribution the station had made to ITN over the years. He wrote: "Without being invidious, people of the calibre of Brian Waddell, Derek Murray, Ivan Little and the others that we at ITN know particularly well, have our unstinted admiration." Brian and Derek were the programme controller and his deputy, so for me to get a mention was quite something.

That same year, ITN asked me to consider going to London to do shifts for them there. Finally, in September 1984, I agreed to fly over on a Saturday morning for a couple of days. I dropped my bags at my hotel and went straight to the ITN offices in central London, where I didn't even get the chance to take off my coat. I was immediately informed I was going out on a big story – to County Cork!

A private jet was waiting at Heathrow to take me and my crew, including the renowned cameraman Sebastian Rich, to where the Navy had captured an IRA gunrunning ship, the *Marita Ann*. It was carrying seven tons of weapons from America. As we flew over the Irish Sea, celebrating my thirty-third birthday with a couple of bottles of champagne on the way, we located the boat and its Navy escorts off the southwest coast. I did a piece-to-camera on the plane and when we landed we edited a package for ITN's early bulletins. That night, we filmed the IRA gunrunners being led off the *Marita Ann*. The Provo in charge was Martin Ferris, now a Sinn Féin deputy in the Irish parliament, Dáil Eireann.

What made the whole experience more surreal was the fact that in 2000, I went to Boston to make a special documentary for UTV about Irish-American John McIntyre. He had been murdered after skippering the boat, the *Valhalla*, which took the arms shipment to rendezvous with Ferris and the others on the *Marita Ann*, off the Irish coast. The people who set up the arms deal for the Provos were an amazing mix of pro-IRA Irish-Americans and Mafia bosses. Unfortunately for McIntyre, he was arrested shortly after his return to Boston over a domestic dispute. He was freed without charge but the gunrunners jumped to the wrong conclusion, believing him to be the spy who tipped off the authorities about the *Marita Ann*. Later on, when I met the IRA informer, Sean O'Callaghan, in London to interview him for the documentary, he admitted that he was the mole who had tipped off his handlers in British Intelligence about the shipment, and they passed on his information to the Irish. O'Callaghan had been a close ally of Martin Ferris and said he had been with him right up until the point where he boarded the *Marita Ann* in Fenit, County Kerry. McIntyre was killed because he had been caught up in the dirty world of spying. The real source of the *Marita Ann* information, O'Callaghan, didn't even know of McIntyre's existence. McIntyre's body was buried in a secret grave and was only discovered in 2000 after one of the Boston mob turned informer and told the FBI.

Sitting in Kerry with Martin Ferris twenty years later, after a performance of *The History of the Troubles (accordin' to my Da)*, was an unreal squaring of a rather sordid circle. I had had tea and fruit cake in Boston with John McIntyre's mother and brother; I'd enjoyed a splendid meal in London with Sean O'Callaghan, and now I was drinking pints in Kerry with Ferris, the man who allegedly led the *Marita Ann* enterprise for the Provos. McIntyre, O'Callaghan and Ferris were a trio, inexorably linked by one of the IRA's most daring, yet ultimately doomed, arms missions. While one had been working for the IRA, and another for British Intelligence, McIntyre had been labouring for his romantic Irish-American ideals in helping to unite Ireland; and he was the one who ended up dead, killed in the mistaken belief that he had betrayed his cause and his paymasters.

When I walked into the ITN offices early on another Saturday morning, three years after the *Marita Ann* affair, the news editor told me he wanted me to cover the capture of, would you believe it, another IRA gun ship: the *Eksund*. Talk about coincidence!

In the mid-80s there was talk of me getting a job with ITN in London, but it wasn't coming from me. It wasn't that I didn't have the ambition for such a post. It was just that complications in my personal life meant I didn't want to leave Northern Ireland and, in particular, Emma. Ivan McMichael's predictions about my marriage had come true: it was over. I had only been with UTV a couple of years when I began seeing someone other than Joan. That relationship developed out of my participation in amateur drama but it wasn't the catalyst for me leaving my wife. That came later, in 1985, after I became involved with my UTV colleague, Kate Smith, and we set up home together. Telling Emma I was leaving was the most difficult thing I have ever had to do, especially since I hadn't a bad word to say about her mum, for whom I still had strong feelings. Informing UTV about the new relationship and trying to keep it out of the tabloids became a major priority. Thankfully in 1985 there was plenty to occupy the newspapers other than my private life. The Anglo-Irish Agreement was signed in November, sparking a major storm among loyalists, and winning me an international award.

The award was for a report on an eventful visit of the then Secretary of State, Tom King, to a function in Belfast's City Hall five days after the agreement was signed. Loyalists, including a raft of politicians who are now household names, were waiting for him at the rear entrance to the City Hall. They included Jeffrey Donaldson, Sammy Wilson and Nigel Dodds. There was utter mayhem as Mr King's minders tried to smuggle him in through a side gate that turned out to be locked. The bodyguards then had to fight their way back with their boss. Some of the crowd threw punches at the government minister. Eventually, the police heavies hustled their boss into the City Hall as the loyalist heavies went crazy outside. There was an action replay of chaos as the Keystone Cops tried to get Mr King out again after his lunch, which can't have been the most pleasant meal he has ever had. On his return, several people, including the firebrand Scottish loyalist George Seawright, tried to get at the Secretary of State again. Seawright, who was jumping up and down like a demented dervish on the official car, was later jailed for his part in the protest. But by far the most famous image of the day was the astonishing sight of a policeman and a DUP politician, Denny Vitty, wrestling with one another in an ornamental flowerpot at the back of the City Hall. Forget the Keystone Cops. This was the stuff of a Laurel and

Hardy caper, and our cameraman, David Scott, didn't miss a second of it. Near the end, Ian Paisley turned up and rounded on me for suggesting that the loyalists had physically attacked Mr King. Surrounded by dozens of his baying supporters, I kept on and on at the DUP leader. I thought they were going to string me up but I managed to escape unscathed.

What made the day's coverage even sweeter was that the BBC missed most of the protest. Even now, all these years later, I still get requests for copies of the report, including one, not so long ago, from Tom King himself! UTV entered the report in the New York International Television Festival without telling me – and it won a silver medal. Just three days after the shenanigans at the back of the City Hall, I returned to the front of the building to cover the story of over 100,000 loyalists protesting against the agreement. That certainly wasn't the last drama arising out of the anti-agreement protests; for instance, there was the time I narrowly missed becoming a human torch.

I had covered the 1986 "invasion" of the County Monaghan border village of Clontibret by the DUP's deputy leader, Peter Robinson, and his supporters. Robinson was arrested and subsequently appeared at Dundalk courthouse where dozens of loyalists turned up for the hearing. Afterwards they strutted back through the staunchly republican town to their cars. I was walking at the front of the crowd interviewing several DUP politicians, including David Calvert, when republicans hiding in the first floor of a derelict building attacked the loyalists underneath. Out of the corner of my eye, I saw something falling from a window and thought I could see flames. When it hit the ground, I heard a *whoosh* and felt a scorching sensation on the back of my neck. The republicans had thrown down a crateful of burning petrol bombs on top of the crowd. Their lethal fireball just missed me by a few inches as it crashed on to the street. I have no doubt that if the crate had been thrown just seconds earlier, it would have killed, or seriously injured, both myself and the people around me. My instant response was not the one normally adopted by war correspondents as they come under fire in far-flung trouble spots, and continue to calmly address the camera in the midst of the mayhem. Er, no. I'm afraid my reaction was to scream, "Fuck me" and run as fast as my long legs would take me, weaving in and out of the riot squads, who were charging into the building to arrest the culprits.

It wasn't the only heat of that long hot summer. The temperatures were also soaring during the Twelfth of July "celebrations". I drew the short straw of going to Portadown to cover the Eleventh Night bonfires. Sure enough, vicious fighting erupted between hundreds of loyalists in the Edgarstown area and dozens of nationalists on the other side of the so-called peace lines in Obins Street. The security forces moved in and took up positions in the nationalist enclave and started firing plastic bullets at the loyalist rioters. For over an hour we stood among the Protestants, dodging the baton rounds and filming the rioters, who were dropping like flies. At one point, a prominent loyalist sidled up to me and calmly asked, "Do you want us to get the shooters out?" Fuck this, I thought. No way was I having anything to do with any of this. I reckoned they were only going to get the shooters out for the cameras. I told my crew to gather up their gear and we cleared off back to our hotel, the Seagoe in Portadown. I knew we could be back within minutes if the trouble did escalate.

I headed off to bed, but my night's sleep didn't last long. At around four in the morning, reception rang to say Billy Wright wanted to see me. Bleary-eyed, I went down to meet him. He wanted me to go with him to Craigavon hospital to see the people injured by plastic bullets. I felt like Mother Teresa as I toured the

Accident and Emergency department, meeting the wounded who eagerly showed me their bruises. On the return to the hotel car park, Wright talked to me for over an hour about himself and about his ideals. He portrayed himself as a loyalist of conscience, a man who didn't want to see anyone dying in the armed struggle.

Wright prophesied his own death during that and subsequent conversations. In one interview he said, "I have only one life and I want to keep it. I am not worried by the IRA. They are common murderers. But I know that it is only a matter of time before I am the victim of a political assassination." He also hinted that the authorities might have a hand in his death. "They are not to be trusted," he said. "I believe there is a conspiracy to kill me, to appease the Dublin government and the republican community." Wright was proved correct inasmuch as he *was* murdered, though not by the IRA. It was the INLA who shot him dead while he sat in a prison van inside the Maze prison, waiting to go on a visit. His father David is convinced that the authorities colluded in his son's killing to ensure a smoother passage for the peace process.

After Billy Wright's murder, his words outside the Seagoe Hotel replayed in my mind. I dug out the tape of the conversation to be certain that Wright had, indeed, foretold his own fate. It must be remembered though that, on that occasion, Wright also said the security forces and the intelligence authorities were blaming him for things he claimed to be innocent of. He insisted to me that they were spreading disinformation about him, alleging he was running his own death squad and suchlike. I knew he was as guilty as sin but I wasn't going to argue with him as he sat beside me in the car, a few miles from where his fellow loyalists had been bragging about their readiness to produce guns. It was ironic too that, for the next few years, the majority of the statements the UVF passed to me about their actions were admissions about murders that Billy Wright had ordered and orchestrated as he and his cohorts carried out a campaign of vicious killings in the mid-Ulster area.

It wasn't just the loyalist killers who made covering death and destruction my staple diet in UTV throughout the 80s. The Provos didn't need to take lessons from anyone in barbarity and brutality. More and more frequently, I found myself rapping on victims' doors, seeking out interviews and responses to the nightmarish atrocities visited upon their loved ones. My attitude to such intrusions was changing. In my early days, I didn't have a problem with trying to persuade relatives to do interviews, especially as the local BBC were using English trainees, like Nicholas Witchell and James Robbins, to cover the stories here. I wanted to match, and outdo these reporters to keep UTV ahead of the game. I thought nothing of bidding farewell to Witchell, particularly at an incident scene, and driving off behind him, then doing a U-turn to go back and get the all-important interview. However, as time wore on, my capacity for hassling the families of victims started to wear thin and I resolved that I would learn to take "no" for an answer. I knew door-stepping would have to go on but I wasn't going to mimic rivals and their offensive patter about how doing interviews helped some people with the grieving process. This was complete and utter crap! Anyway, as my face became better known, I didn't have to launch into an introduction. If people wanted to talk to me, they would invite me in. If they didn't want to chat, they were usually polite and just asked me to leave them alone.

Rarely have I felt more humble and readier to turn away from a house than at the home of Gordon Wilson. He lost his daughter Marie in the Enniskillen massacre in November 1987, when the IRA bombed a Remembrance Day service at the town's cenotaph, killing a total of eleven people. What made the tragedy even more upsetting for me was the fact that when the bomb exploded, I was at the cenotaph in Whitehall with Emma on one of our regular outings to London. I don't know why I took her there as I had never been to a Remembrance service anywhere before. When I heard that Marie Wilson had died by her father's side I couldn't help envisaging Emma and myself in a similar situation.

By the time I reached the Wilsons' home, he had already conducted a lengthy series of interviews about the bombing. A relative answered the front door and told me Mr Wilson wasn't up to any more meetings with the press. I wasn't going to argue and turned to leave. Suddenly Gordon Wilson appeared, saying, "Sure, we can't leave UTV out, can we?" He then ushered me into his front room. For the umpteenth time, and with no less emotion, he recounted to me how Marie had whispered the words, "Daddy, I love you very much" just before she died. That triggered my tears. I explained to him that hearing his story made me imagine Emma and myself in a similar situation in London. The meeting ended up with *him* comforting *me*. His wife Joan came into the room to offer us tea and scones. I thought we had been a big enough burden already and said thanks but no thanks, explaining that we had to hurry on to somewhere else. She insisted that it was no trouble and that she would feel slighted if we didn't have a cuppa. So we stayed and I can't honestly remember a more welcome brew. Many years later, during rehearsals for *The History of the Troubles*, one of the most difficult challenges for me was making the switch from comedy to tragedy at the mention of the Enniskillen bomb. It wasn't until I started to think about the devastated yet dignified Wilson home and the moving funeral for Marie that I was able to make the transition convincing.

The week after the Enniskillen bomb was a non-stop procession of pain, with funeral after funeral on day after day. Sadly, I think I have probably covered more funerals than any other journalist in Northern Ireland. RTE's now retired cameraman, Johnny Coghlan, always maintained that between us we had attended the majority of funerals during the troubles.

As a newspaper reporter, it was easy to melt into the background; but when accompanied by a camera crew I initially felt like a complete waste of space, intruding on grieving families as they buried their loved ones. There was nowhere for journalists and cameramen like Johnny and I to hide as we openly watched and recorded the families and mourners' every move and every tear. It didn't matter who was involved, the grief was exactly the same. The victim may have been a civilian claimed by sectarianism, a policeman murdered by a no-warning bomb, or a terrorist killed by the security forces – or by his own hand. Regardless of who the deceased was, the relatives all displayed the same raw emotions.

For some inexplicable reason, one funeral out of all the hundreds I have attended still plays in my mind as if it were yesterday. Robin Shields, who had been in the police reserve, was shot dead by the IRA in September 1980. He died at his desk in the ambulance depot of the Royal Victoria Hospital. The grief as his coffin was brought from his home in the Woodvale area of Belfast was so overpowering, so intense, that I had to walk away. To cap it all, a series of IRA bomb scares held up the funeral, causing some mourners to miss the burial at Roselawn cemetery.

The longer the troubles dragged on the more I had to steel myself to the sorrow and sadness. I had a job to do, after all. Most journalists from here, including myself, have always tried to show respect for the mourning families and there were times when I felt like thumping visiting hacks as they descended on funerals. I remember one occasion in particular. It was the funeral of young plastic bullet victim, Seamus Duffy, in north Belfast in 1989. Scores of photographers and camera crews from every corner of the globe were in Belfast at the time to cover the twentieth anniversary of the start of the troubles. One obnoxious American photographer actually lay on the ground in the path leading from the Duffy house, intending to take a picture of the coffin going over him. I almost applauded when one of our local snappers dragged the baseball-capped Yank away by the scruff of the neck. The American was later charged with having bomb parts in his car. Several years later, he was killed while on assignment in the former Yugoslavia.

1989 also saw one of my most surreal markings, which had nothing to do with the troubles: it was the Kegworth air disaster, in which forty-seven people were killed near East Midlands Airport in England. My evening started with the singer Paul Brady serenading me as I stood in a queue of people unlucky not to get tickets for his gig at the Parador hotel in Belfast. After this impromptu performance, the girl I was seeing at the time suggested we drive to a bar in Cushendall, forty miles away, for a jar. I was just getting the drinks in when my news editor, Colm McWilliams, made contact to ask me to cover the air crash.

"We are trying to hire a light aircraft," he said. "Where are you?" I knew if I told the truth, Colm would find someone else to go. "I'm in the house," I lied, grabbing my hapless companion. We broke every speed limit in the land to get back to Belfast for a change of clothes while en route to work.

"The car wouldn't start," I lied again. I then set off for Newtownards airport, where a pilot was waiting with a four-seater plane to fly my crew and me across the Irish Sea. As the rain and the wind was bouncing off the plane we weren't particularly happy on take-off. The pilot further increased our anxiety by asking my colleague, Albert Kirk, to shut the aircraft's door, as it wasn't closed properly. Not what the doctor ordered for my shattered nerves! Anyway we got there safely and at Liverpool airport, thanks to the connivance of a sympathetic security guard, we "hijacked" a hire car, hotwiring it to take us to the crash site.

We went straight to a hospital in Nottingham, where we found survivors and relatives of the injured from Northern Ireland. We worked through the night and, first thing in the morning, a Welshman called Gareth Jones, who lived and worked in Northern Ireland, appeared at a news conference to talk about how he and seventy-eight others survived the crash. I was the only hack from this side of the Irish Sea at the conference and, as he was wheeled away, Gareth asked to speak to me. Tearfully, he told me how lovely it had been to hear a Northern Irish accent and how it had cheered him up.

A crisis loomed in Nottingham when I discovered I couldn't get any editing facilities there. I raced to Birmingham to catch a flight to Belfast, where I cut a nine minute package for the UTV tea-time news. Afterwards, I returned to Newtownards to collect my car from the airfield. After driving for a few minutes I had to stop the car. I was so exhausted and befuddled with all the travelling and lack of sleep that I didn't have a clue where I was. It was the only time that had ever happened to me, apart from the occasional mists of drunkenness. I sat in a blind panic for a little while before it occurred to me to look for a road sign. For once, I was pleased to see that Belfast was a few short miles away.

CHAPTER 9

The Bookies, the Bastards and the "Bad Bet"

The 1990s were to prove a crucial decade for Northern Ireland in the search for peace; and also for me, in my search for peace of mind. My relationship with Kate Smith crumbled after four years, a situation made more awkward by the fact that we sat right next to each other in the newsroom. However, it's fair to say that, in 1989, I wasn't exactly living the lonely life of a recluse. I didn't have far to travel from my newly acquired apartment to one of my favourite drinking destinations in south Belfast, the Wellington Park Hotel. Friday nights were party nights and the place had become legendary. The visiting ITN crews, with whom I worked at weekends, refused to stay anywhere else. Furthermore, one English soccer team used to come to Belfast for pre-season tours simply because their manager loved to sample the Friday night pleasures of the "Welly", where even the worst striker in the land could score. I used to get stick from my mates that the only reason I liked going there was because my ugly face was regularly on television. Honestly though: a balding, overweight one-legged midget with bad breath and a hunched back could have pulled in the "Welly", and that was on a bad night.

One of the women I met there proved to be more than a one-night stand. Michelle Savage was a successful solicitor who became pregnant by me and gave birth to a baby girl, Claire, in July 1990. In the midst of my messed-up world at the time, I knew the relationship with Michelle was unlikely to survive the madness. I found it difficult to face up to my new responsibilities. Fortunately, with time, I was able to grow up and to be there for Claire, who is now a bright, feisty, drama-loving teenager. But back in 1990, I knew I had to get my life straightened out. If I didn't slow down, the Friday night frolics, along with ongoing excesses on the merry-go-round of amateur drama, would catch up with me one way or another. So I decided to get out of Belfast altogether and rented a small house in Holywood, County Down with the intention of settling down and wising up.

But fate is an ironic bugger. On my very first night in Holywood, I resolved to have a quiet night in, alone, all by myself. That was my honest intention; but then a friend from UTV, Stephen McCoubrey, called to say hello – and we went up the town for a jar, just the one. You can imagine my supreme horror at ending up, finally, in the "Welly". I'm still not sure whose fault that was, but I'm certain it wasn't mine! However, within minutes of arriving, I spied a girl called Siofra O'Reilly. She had been a set designer with one of my old amateur drama groups, the Circle, and quickly became aware of my designs on her. Fifteen years later, we are still together. What makes the whole thing even more ironic is that Siofra and I had virtually been neighbours in Belfast: just a few hundred yards separated our homes. Yet, it wasn't until that night, after my moving eight miles away from Belfast, that we bumped into each other for the first time.

Meanwhile, relationships of a different kind were developing in the outside world, with reports that the IRA and the British government were sounding each other out to find a way out of the Ulster impasse. On the streets you would never have guessed this. The Provos seemed intent on exploding even bigger bombs while the UFF, under the direction of Johnny Adair, and the UVF, especially in mid-Ulster under Billy Wright's guidance, were ruthlessly gunning down Catholics. The more the terrorists talked of peace, the more their actions spoke of war. And it only got worse.

In January 1992, the IRA exploded a bomb at Teebane in County Tyrone. It killed eight Protestant workmen returning from a military base they had been refurbishing. I heard about the blast while on holiday in Spain and my first reaction was that I was glad to be out of it. Still, there was to be no escape from the next massacre on the terrorists' bloody agenda, the UFF's revenge for Teebane.

On that fateful Wednesday – February 5, 1992 – I was driving up the Ormeau Road heading for the RUC headquarters at Knock. I was working on a report about a policeman who had gone on a murderous rampage the previous day. He had shot three civilians at the Sinn Féin offices on the Falls Road before turning the gun on himself. However, his demented killing spree was about to be overtaken in barbarity, right in front of my eyes.

As I travelled up the Ormeau Road, people were running towards Sean Graham's bookmakers' shop. On my right, I spotted a clearly distressed local woman, Joyce McCartan, who had lost many members of her immediate family in the troubles. She shouted at me through her tears, "They've killed eight or nine people in the bookies." I stopped the car and sprinted across the road just as police were arriving on the scene – a scene of blood and chaos. People lay dead or wounded on the floor of the bookies. Dazed and distraught survivors staggered outside for air. UTV colleague, Marty Gibson, was quickly at my side, filming this snapshot from hell. Men lay helpless on the pavement with many more people emerging from the bookies covered in blood. I stood still, in shock.

Through all my years on the frontline of the troubles, I had never seen anything quite like this. Journalists normally arrive at shootings and bombings after the dust has settled and even then we are held back behind police lines. This was a stark contrast, an assault on all my senses. So much was happening all around us, it was almost impossible to take it all in. Marty, however, missed nothing as the paramedics ferried the injured out on stretchers in a neverending conveyor belt. Even more heartbreaking was the sight of relatives arriving on the road to find out about their loved ones. One of my most distressing memories is watching one young man running up to the bookies to be told the worst about his father, and then listening to his cry of anguish. It was one of the few sounds I remember from that day. I had often heard from witnesses to terror attacks about the silence of the immediate aftermath; and right enough, on the Ormeau Road, an eerie stillness descended on the streets as dozens of people gathered to watch. No one screamed out for revenge and no one shouted out abuse about the loyalist killers. Just a stunned air of hopeless despair hung over the road. My own senses were numb. I remember thinking that it all seemed so unreal, although that changed several hours later when I sat down at home to watch a tape of my report. It might sound daft, but it was only through watching the TV pictures of what had happened that the reality of the atrocity hit home and I broke down at the insanity and waste of it all. Five people had died, including a teenage boy.

Shortly afterwards, a relative of one of the victims came to see me at UTV with a special plea. In my news report, we showed his badly injured relative emerging from the bookies on a stretcher and it had now been established that he had actually passed away between leaving Grahams and arriving at the ambulance. The man asked me to stop using the footage, which I did without a second thought.

Seeing the massacre at such close range was terrible enough but hearing some of the reactions to it made my blood boil. A number of heartless animals actually rang radio programmes and wrote to newspapers to ask what a teenage boy had been doing in the bookies in the first place. No condemnation of the killers; no sympathy for the families. It was appalling. Worse was to come. On July 8, five months later, an Orange march made its way down the Ormeau Road, past the bookies. Some of the loyalists shouted, "Up the UFF." Others held up one of their hands, showing five fingers, one for each of the victims. The then Secretary of State, Sir Patrick Mayhew, said the actions would have disgraced a tribe of cannibals.

Nationalists and republicans would deny it, but the cannibals would have disowned many of their actions too. Who will ever forget the images of the hate-filled mobs that dragged two soldiers from their car and murdered them after they strayed into an IRA funeral in 1988? Not that the security forces are exactly blameless either. I've heard the snide asides of police officers at funerals to the relatives of republicans who have been killed "in action", as the IRA call it. Then there was the obscene mocking by Paratroopers who, after they had killed Martin Peake and Karen Reilly in a stolen car in west Belfast in 1990, built a replica of their vehicle and put up a sign reading VAUXHALL ASTRA: BUILT BY ROBOTS. DRIVEN BY JOYRIDERS. STOPPED BY "A" COMPANY. Maybe it's because I have seen so much grief, in so many homes of so many people from so many different backgrounds, that I despise every last one of those who deal and delight in death. How anyone can be so sick, so twisted and so hard-hearted as to take pleasure in someone else's pain and suffering is, quite simply, beyond me. My blood has run cold listening to spokesmen for terrorist groups boast about killings, excusing themselves by blaming the other side for starting it all.

In October 1993, the IRA tried to talk their way out of one such appalling act of violence, the Shankill Road bombing. They said they had been "merely" trying to kill members of the UFF, including Johnny Adair, and not the nine innocent civilians who died in the blast. So that was OK then? I arrived on the Shankill not long after the explosion. Rescuers were still trying to dig people out of the rubble that had been Frizzell's fish shop. The IRA claimed the bomb was designed to kill UFF members who had been meeting in offices directly above the shop, offices that Belfast journalists knew well from countless visits to hear statements from the organisation. The UFF had, indeed, been using the building for meetings but not when the bomb exploded, on an eleven-second timer. Among the dead was an IRA bomber, Thomas Begley. Incredibly, his colleague, Sean Kelly, survived.

Shortly afterwards, a Protestant man, who also survived the blast, told me how Kelly had been rushed to the Mater hospital in the same ambulance as himself and a young relative. He described to me how he had, unwittingly, befriended Kelly in the ambulance, talking to him and reassuring him that he would be alright. He now said he wanted to kill him. Over the next weeks and months, he contacted me from time to time, thoroughly fixated with the idea of exacting his revenge on the man he had helped in that ambulance. He said he dreamt of getting a gun and going to the hospital where Kelly was recovering. The RUC were well aware of his plans and reckoned the more he talked about it, the less likely he was to do it.

The week after the Shankill bombing was one of the most frightening periods I have ever encountered during the troubles. Everyone knew that the UFF would launch a major revenge attack but no one knew where or when it would come. Several people died in a series of gun attacks within days but the security forces braced themselves for what they called a "spectacular". In Belfast, few people went out at night as tension gripped the city. By the end of the week, I couldn't take it any longer. Siofra and I headed to Enniskillen for a Halloween weekend break, thinking that it would be a safe haven. During a relaxing dinner in a local restaurant, my boss Colm McWilliams called to tell me that the UFF had just killed seven people in a bar not far from Derry.

I had never heard of Greysteel, but I was there the following morning to report on the callous gun attack on the Rising Sun bar. Terrorists had shouted, "Trick or Treat", before opening fire with an AK-47 rifle and a 9mm automatic pistol. As I went in search of survivors and relatives of the dead, I realized again how small a place Northern Ireland really is. At one house which had lost a loved one a woman invited me in, telling me it wasn't the first time I had been there. She pointed across the road to a field and said, "You called here looking for directions the time Richard Branson hit the ground over there." She was referring to the time in 1987, when Branson's cross-Atlantic balloon briefly brushed the ground before he had to ditch his craft near Rathlin Island. "Mr Branson always said he would build a monument here," she added. "But we are still waiting."

Now, a different sort of memorial stands in Greysteel, a simple plaque with the names of the people who died on that terrible night. Something else from that massacre that stays with me, and countless others, is the spectacle of the Greysteel killers emerging from court in Limavady just days after the shooting. One of them, Torrens Knight was dragged to a police car screaming UFF slogans and laughing like a maniac. A more poignant image was John Hume weeping at the funerals after a woman mourner stepped forward to thank him for what he had done in his quest for peace. This quest, to a hardened cynic like myself, seemed even less likely to succeed in the dark days of 1993.

The beginning of 1994 wasn't any more inspiring, though people were insisting to me that republicans were inching positively along the path to peace. That didn't exactly tally with their murder of a bloke I had known for years. Jackie Haggan was a friend of a friend of mine, and had attended my stag night in 1974. He was a cop by profession but his real passion was greyhound racing. He was taking one hell of a risk in going to the races at Dunmore Stadium in north Belfast, although friends say he always took precautions. Still, the Provos cut him down in front of his pregnant wife in the lounge of the stadium. Seven weeks later, the UVF retaliated by killing a newsagent in Belfast. As they passed on their statement of admission to me, I knew that this was the last thing Jackie would have wanted.

Sandwiched between the two murders was one of the most savage and senseless killings it has ever been my misfortune to report on, the slaying of Margaret Wright in April 1994. It was so repugnant that I decided to make a special half-hour documentary about it. My main source of information was Frankie Curry, a veteran loyalist assassin who, police believed, killed one of the people suspected of Margaret Wright's murder. Curry was high up in the Red Hand Commando and met me regularly to give me chapter and verse about the killing. He also ordered other RHC members to co-operate with me.

Miss Wright, a thirty-one year old Protestant woman, had gone for a late night drink to the seedy "Bad Bet" drinking club, off the Donegall Road in Belfast. The all-night shebeen was run by a loyalist flute band associated with the Red Hand Commando, a UVF-aligned terror group. It seems that Margaret's questions about terrorist plaques on the walls led people in the club to believe she was a Catholic. Her denials were ignored and she was beaten with pool cues and a brush shaft before being shot in the head. Her killers then put her naked body in a wheelie bin and pushed it half a mile to dump it at the back of a derelict house. It was discovered twenty hours later by police.

A few days later the UVF killed one of their own, Ian Hamilton. He had fired the four fatal shots that had taken Margaret Wright's life. A number of other men were jailed for their part in the killing. Police had no doubt that the ringleader was RHC boss, Billy Elliott, but he didn't crack under interrogation and no one would testify against him. He was never charged and fled to Scotland until he believed it safe to return. But Elliott had reckoned without Frankie Curry. In September 1995, Curry shot Elliott not far from his own home in Bangor. In 1999, Curry boasted to journalists that Elliott was one of at least nineteen people he had killed. Curry, a nephew of the former UVF killer Gusty Spence, was himself shot dead on the Shankill Road by his erstwhile colleagues a couple of days after his newspaper interviews. I once asked him why he, a ruthless and hardened murderer, was so keen to help me with the Margaret Wright documentary. "It's one thing to shoot a man," he said. "But it's not on to kill a wee girl." What he didn't concede was that his concern might just have been solely based on the fact that Margaret was a Protestant. It might have proved an altogether different story if she *had* been the Catholic her killers believed her to be.

That was certainly the thinking of Armagh man Frank Smyth, whose Catholic daughter Anne-Marie had been slaughtered in 1992 in almost identical circumstances. She had strayed into a loyalist club in east Belfast. In an interview for the Margaret Wright documentary, Mr Smyth told me he believed the outrage over the Donegall Road murder had been intensified because of the mistake over Margaret's religion. He contended that, because his daughter *was* a Catholic, there had been nowhere near as big an outcry after her throat had been cut and her body dumped on waste ground.

During the making of that programme I came across two disturbing coincidences. Margaret's funeral, in April 1994, was the first to be conducted in the new £5-million Metropolitan Tabernacle church on the Shore Road. It had been opened seven weeks earlier by the colourful preacher, Pastor James McConnell. I decided to review UTV's pictures of the opening ceremony and, within minutes, I saw Margaret standing beside our camera among the thousands of worshippers, singing with outstretched arms.

The second coincidence came when I interviewed Margaret's mother at Roselawn cemetery after one of her weekly visits to lay flowers on her daughter's grave. As I walked back to my car, I suddenly noticed that just a few rows away from Margaret's last resting place was the grave and headstone of Billy Elliott, the man who had ordered her murder.

It wasn't surprising that, in the wake of Margaret Wright's murder, there would be the usual calls on the paramilitaries to desist, disband and disappear. It was equally unsurprising to me that the paramilitaries wouldn't listen to those demands, and both sides were soon butchering people again, with the UFF being particularly busy and brutal. Then, in June 1994, the INLA triggered another massacre by shooting three prominent loyalists on the Shankill Road after a UVF meeting. The loyalists took just two days to seek their revenge. They killed six Catholic men in a quiet country pub at Loughinisland in County Down as they sat watching Ireland play Italy in a World Cup soccer match.

On that night I was at a Grosvenor High School reunion when I got the call to go to Loughinisland. The following morning, as with Greysteel, I had to ask directions to Loughinisland because I had never heard of the place. It was a journey I was to make repeatedly over the next few days as I covered the funerals in this quiet little hamlet, too small to call a village. Yet again, it was difficult to fend off feelings of despair for the future as loyalists threatened to surpass every republican atrocity with even bigger and bloodier reprisals.

Billy Wright had once explained the loyalist thinking to me. They believed that the IRA would have to realise that, if they wanted to continue their war against Britain and the unionists in Northern Ireland, they must be prepared to see more and more innocent Catholics become victims. When the IRA called a ceasefire on August 31, 1994 Wright and other paramilitaries were convinced their tactics of "payback terror" had forced the Provos into a virtual surrender. Few observers agreed with the loyalists' analysis, pointing to the years of planning and positioning which preceded the ceasefire announcement, long before the UVF and the UFF had embarked on their vengeful massacres.

The big question now was whether or not the loyalist terrorists would announce a ceasefire of their own. The messages coming from the paramilitaries were mixed. Just before the Provos called a halt, the Combined Loyalist Military Command (CLMC), which represented the main loyalist groups, issued a statement saying they would respond positively to an IRA cessation. However, as the weeks went on, there were conflicting signals with some of the paramilitaries playing hard ball. My money was firmly on the Prods ultimately following the Provo lead, but not before they had sunk again into the most grotesque gutters.

CHAPTER 10

Prodding the Paramilitaries
on to Peace

No one wanted peace more than me; I was utterly sick and tired of the violence. On the other hand, I could scarcely have been more cynical about the prospects for a lasting settlement. By the middle of the 90s, I had lost count of how many killings I had covered but I knew that it ran into the hundreds. After all the massacres of the early 90s, I was fairly sure that nothing else could shock me, and then two more killings, and their repercussions in court, smashed my complacency.

Now, close and all as I had been to murders and bombings, I had never actually seen anyone being killed until I went into court to cover the trial of Thomas McWilliams. He was charged with the 1993 IRA murder of Protestant shopkeeper, Norman Truesdale. Everyone in the Crumlin Road courthouse, which was only a few yards away from the victim's shop, watched in shocked silence while officials played the recording of the shooting. It had been captured by a security camera above the victim's head. I was struck by how the taking of a life was all so mundane, so matter-of-fact. Somehow, after watching people being killed in movies, you expect it to be high-octane, high drama. But, here we watched Norman Truesdale serve a boy at the counter with crisps and chocolate when, calm as you like, two masked men walked into the shop. The first killer shot him with a handgun and after Mr Truesdale slumped to the floor, the second killer fired more shots into him with his rifle. I timed how long the killers had been in the shop: four and a half seconds. Mr Truesdale has subsequently been linked to loyalist murder gangs, but his killing was breathtakingly brutal.

I knew Mr Truesdale's shop well from my childhood. It was on the Oldpark Road, at its junction with Century Street, where one of my mother's best friends, Sadie Norris, lived with her husband Bob. We visited them regularly for Sunday evening teas and Christmas meals. That little shop's troubles had actually started years earlier. Its previous owner, Billy Quee, a leading figure in the UDA, was shot dead by the Irish People's Liberation Organisation (IPLO) in September 1988. Century Street must have been one of the shortest streets in Belfast and it later gained even more notoriety when a book about UFF leader, Johnny "Mad Dog" Adair, said it was where he and his friends used to gather every evening when they were younger.

Long after the Truesdale court case ended, I frequently thought about the killing. One of Norman Truesdale's relatives, who had spoken to me at the courthouse, kept in contact with me. She described how his death had shattered her life and she found herself even trying to sleep beside his grave to be closer to him.

The Crumlin Road courthouse was also where I watched another horror being played out, though not on video. This one was happening right in front of me. I was in court for the conclusion of the trial of the four men who had been charged in connection with the murder of a twenty year old Catholic man. Sean Monaghan had been abducted by the UFF in August 1994.

Mr Monaghan, whose partner was a Protestant girl, had managed to escape from his captors. They had been holding him in a house in Disraeli Street. However, after seeking help from a pensioner, he ended up back in his kidnappers' hands, and they shot him dead.

The agony of Sean Monaghan's family was made even worse in court. The judge, Lord Justice Nicholson, convicted the four men on charges related to the murder, which he described as being one of the most brutal and cruel he had ever encountered. He added that we might never know who had actually fired the fatal shots. This sparked the most frightening demonstration of naked sectarian hatred I have ever witnessed – and I've seen a few, believe me. One of the men in the dock, David Burrows, leapt up and started screaming at the Monaghan family as he pretended to fire an imaginary gun: "I shot your son. Four in the back of the fucking head. Up the UFF!" The judge immediately ordered Burrows to be removed from the court. He had to allow him back for his sentencing, whereupon Burrows yelled more obscenities at the stricken family, adding that he was proud to be a member of the UFF's second battalion. "We'll win the war. I shot him," he roared. The only response from the victim's family was a whisper from his mother. Anne Monaghan looked at Burrows through her tears and said, "I hope you see my son's face every day for the rest of your life."

Outside the court, police had to provide protection for the Monaghans, hustling them into Land Rovers, as loyalists hurled abuse at them. It was awful. I followed the Monaghans to their west Belfast home to get their reaction on tape. Anne Monaghan told me the goading and the gloating had been completely unexpected, and was devastating. She said, "Mr Burrows is an evil man. He should be locked away for life and he should never get out of prison. I will hate him to the day I die and I hope he will end up climbing the walls in an asylum." She revealed that, during the trial, she had actually started to feel sorry for the four men in the dock because she thought it was possible that they had been unwittingly led into the killing by others. But she said any pity she had vanished after her ordeal in the courtroom.

The bitter irony was that Sean Monaghan had been coldly murdered within a few days of the IRA announcing their ceasefire in the summer of 1994, when the loyalists were supposedly weighing up their response to the Provos' move.

The Combined Loyalist Military Command finally announced a ceasefire in October 1994, just before Burrows and his friends were sentenced. While listening to Gusty Spence announce the UVF ceasefire with the words, "In all sincerity, we offer to the loved ones of all innocent victims over the past twenty-five years, abject and true remorse", David Burrows' venomous diatribe at the Monaghans echoed in my head. Clearly not all loyalists concurred with the sentiments.

The night before the CLMC news conference, Brian Rowan, security correspondent for the BBC, and myself had been urged to attend a meeting with political representatives of the paramilitary organisations to discuss what they promised was a momentous development from loyalists. We naturally assumed we were going to be handed a ceasefire statement because the UVF and the UFF usually released their major communiqués to Brian and/or me. Instead we were told that the announcement would be released at a news conference the following morning, thus allowing the world's media an equal crack at the story. After the hassles we had been through over the years, neither Brian nor myself were exactly keen on sharing the story with anyone else. Eventually a compromise was agreed, whereby Brian and I would be given the CLMC statement early the next morning before the other hacks, so that we could run flashes on our early bulletins and break the news of the ceasefire. That duly happened but unfortunately my release of the statement landed my UTV employers in hot water because our newsroom broke into GMTV's air-time to announce the news of the ceasefire. This was forbidden under broadcasting legislation but I didn't know that. UTV were subsequently hauled over the coals. Mea culpa.

The loyalist initiative did little to dispel my reservations about the durability of peace. I bet my old mate, Deric Henderson – by now the editor of the Press Association in Ireland – that it would all fall apart. Stupidly, I agreed to a deadline and when that passed peacefully, I had to fork out my ton. Of course Henderson wouldn't budge when I asked him for a refund after the Provisional's ceasefire collapsed with the Canary Wharf bombing in February 1996.

Of all the interviews I conducted in the aftermath of the earlier loyalist ceasefire about the potential for lasting peace, the most bizarre came in the imposing shape of Roddy McDonald. He was a leader of the UDA in Scotland during the 70s and called himself "The Tartan Warrior". McDonald, who had been jailed for arms and drugs offences, appeared regularly on TV programmes, bragging about the UDA's strength on the mainland but, later on, he retreated into the background. I bumped into him, in the Outer Hebrides, of all places.

In 1995, I had taken Emma with me on a visit to see my sister Caroline and her family in the Hebrides, or the Western Isles, to give them their more modern name. My brother-in-law Robin had taken up a job as head of the local health board. While I was there, I decided to record some features for UTV on Irish people living in that beautiful part of the world. One day, as my cameraman shot some pictures of the harbour in Tarbert on the island of Harris, I saw a face I thought I recognised. It was Roddy McDonald. We chatted and he told me all about himself and his past. He felt the peace process was the only way forward now for Northern Ireland. He agreed to record an interview which ran for five minutes on *UTV Live*, using archive pictures that I unearthed of him in the UDA headquarters in Belfast twenty years earlier. Weird or what?

McDonald said the gun was no longer the answer, but some republicans and loyalists back home clearly didn't agree. In mid-Ulster, Billy Wright's UVF unit carried on killing. They murdered Catholic taxi driver, Michael McGoldrick, in Lurgan at the height of the Drumcree stand-off in 1996. The killing was to be seen as a birthday present for the terrorist leader and the slaying sparked a major and irreparable split in the loyalist camp. That same summer there were also reports of a split within the Provisional IRA, which I unwittingly became caught up in.

Newspaper reports said that a new breakaway group had been formed by Provos in South Derry, South Armagh and East Tyrone and they were opposed to the ceasefire. I was among a number of journalists who received a call from a man claiming to be a spokesman for the dissidents. He said he and his colleagues were going to prove there was a split, and told us to meet him in Armagh. He led us on a wild goose chase around the border region, saying we were going to meet a unit of the new grouping. However, the locations kept changing for what he claimed were security reasons. Later – much, much later – in a forest somewhere outside Carrickmacross, our contact vanished. Then a masked man appeared in paramilitary garb to read out a statement which said that there was, indeed, a chasm in the Provisionals. I exchanged raised eyebrows with the other hacks and we all seemed to be wondering the same thing. Was this man in uniform not just the disappearing guide? The whole thing felt daft and Sinn Féin dismissed it as a stunt inspired by British Intelligence. The next night I was taken in the back of a van to an unknown location in

From Little acorns…
Pictured in the back garden
of 34 Connsbrook Avenue,
1951.

What a spectacle! No, it's not
Roy Orbison – it's me at
Grosvenor High School, 1964.

A piece of cake. Celebrating my twenty-first birthday with my Mum, Iola, and my father, Billy, in Abbey Gardens.

Victor Gordon of the Portadown Times *is over the moon after the town's Irish Cup soccer win over Linfield, 1972. The victory signs are from editor David Armstrong. The hair is all mine.*

My Belfast Telegraph *leaving do in McGlade's pub, 1977. Foreground: the late Ivor McNeilly, Louis McConnell, Billy Simpson (kneeling), me and Neil Johnston. Background: Chris Kelly, Lawrence White and the late John Wallace.*

Yule TV. A Christmas card from UTV, circa 1981. From left to right: Leslie Dawes, Dave Turner, Gerry Kelly, Hilary Bryans, Ian Sanderson, Mike Catto, Jackie Fullerton, me, Raymond Maxwell, Judy Fetherstone, Michael MacMillan, Gloria Hunniford, Hugh Owens and Jeanie Johnston.

Having a ball. Pictured at a charity soccer event during a Northern Ireland international at Windsor Park. The so-called celebs include, from left to right, Gerry Anderson, Tracey-Anne Griffiths, Jim Platt, May McFettridge, John Daly, Wendy Austin and Gerry Kelly.

The Am-Dram Maguire. With members of the Clarence Players after winning the All-Ireland amateur drama trophy in Athlone, 1990. Director Paddy Ormonde is pictured in the centre.

On stage at the Grand Opera House in Belfast after winning the James Young award for best actor in the Ulster drama final, 1990.

Preaching in the shadow of Belfast's Black Man, Dr Henry Cooke, I rehearse for the Centre Stage production of Sam Thompson's play The Evangelist *in 1997.*

My alter ego King Crumble, Su Pollard, May McFettridge and Gladiator Scorpio go on a royal walkabout to promote our Jack and the Beanstalk *pantomime.*

Carey Gold: Singer Mariah Carey tries to butter me up before our interview in a Dublin hotel, 1999.

It's a Phee-non-aanum

It's all right every night with UTV

UTV

utvinternet.com

DUP leader, the Rev Ian Paisley gets a grip as I quiz him about doing a deal with Sinn Féin during the election count in Ballymoney, 2003.

My interview with Gerry Adams in west Belfast, 1992, as captured in paint by Flora McDonnell. (By kind permission of UTV)

Prime Minister Tony Blair's wife Cherie presents my daughter Emma with her diploma on her graduation from the London Academy of Music and Dramatic Art, 1999. Applauding in the background is Sir Timothy West, the LAMDA patron.

The then Secretary of State John Reid and his wife Carine meet the cast and writers of The History of the Troubles *(accordin' to my Da): Conor Grimes, me, Alan McKee and Martin Lynch, 2002.*

Tyrone where two masked IRA men read out a genuine Provo statement rubbishing what had happened the day before.

Some weeks later, at the start of August, I was driven blindfolded to a meeting with the UVF and they made no attempt to paper over the cracks in their organisation. It was the biggest show of strength I had ever seen from them. No fewer than nine masked men were in the room with, at least, the same number of guns on display. A statement from the organisation's command staff was read out, which said they had disbanded a unit of the UVF in Portadown. Within hours, the UVF in mid-Ulster released their first statement. They claimed that the organisation's leaders in Belfast were planning to attack their top men in Portadown – in other words, Billy Wright.

Just a couple of weeks later, I was called to a meeting of political allies of the CLMC. They produced a statement, saying that the mid-Ulster UVF had breached the ceasefire and the CLMC was ordering them to stand down. They also issued a warning to Billy Wright and another man, Alex Kerr. They had exactly seventy-two hours to leave Northern Ireland or face what was called "summary justice". Wright wouldn't back down. The next day, he did an interview and said he was staying put. Wright and his allies then formed the Loyalist Volunteer Force (LVF); it took over where the UVF in mid-Ulster had left off. In March 1997, Wright was jailed for eight years for threatening to kill a Portadown woman. As chance would have it, I was sitting only a few feet away from the dock on the day he was convicted. He kept up a running conversation with me, telling me he had been framed and that he wasn't getting any justice in court. Eventually he shouted at the judge, "Why don't you just intern us?" Lord Justice McCollum responded by having him thrown out of court. That was the last time I saw Billy Wright. By the following Christmas, he was dead, killed by the INLA inside the Maze.

In the same winter, another blast from my Portadown past resurfaced. Roy "RJ" Kerr rang to say he wanted to do a one-off interview with me after his home had been gutted in an arson attack. He claimed the LVF had torched his home because they believed he had led a thirty-strong UVF mob in an attack on one of their bars in Portadown. He said, "The men who burnt my home are the scum of the earth. I have been on terrorist offences. I have been a thief. I have always been a gangster all my life but I done my bit for Ulster." It was to prove to be his epitaph and he became the latest in the long line of terrorists I had known to die. He apparently died by his own hand. It was said that he started a fire on a boat in Warrenpoint and blew himself up in the process. Kerr, who was an associate of the loyalist assassin, Robin "The Jackal" Jackson, was suspected of involvement in countless bombings and shootings but he wasn't only a paramilitary. He was also, as he admitted himself, a thug. One of the first court cases I covered in Belfast was one where Kerr got banged up for running a protection number on a Chinese restaurant in Portadown.

Within six months of Kerr's death, it started to look, even to cynics like me, as if the extremists had had their day. At Stormont I gaped as Ian Paisley was given a rough and foul-mouthed ride by loyalists on the eve of the completion of the Good Friday Agreement. It was signed, sealed and ostensibly delivered on April 10, 1998. The signs were good and voters in a referendum backed the agreement. Still, I couldn't shake a nagging feeling that it was all too good to be true. Dissidents on both sides started to crawl out of the woodwork and the Real IRA launched their bombing campaign. In fact, I was to come dangerously close to one of their devices.

I had been covering Drumcree in 1998 when I was told that the Real IRA had abandoned a bomb near Blackwatertown in County Armagh. The instructions were accurate and, eventually, my

cameraman and I found a covered trailer in a lane, just as the
terrorists had described to us. They also told us that the bomb was
no longer primed. Stupidly, I did a piece to camera right beside
the trailer. Amid the headline-grabbing goings-on at Drumcree
our discovery attracted very little attention. But I broke out in a
cold sweat a couple of days later when the security forces
confirmed that the trailer had contained a massive 1500 pound
bomb, and this lunatic had stood right beside it. If I had ever
needed proof of the power that such a bomb could unleash, I got
it just over a month later.

On August 15, 1998 a similar Real IRA bomb *did* explode with
catastrophic results in the town of Omagh. Twenty-nine people,
including a pregnant woman who was expecting twins, were killed
in the worst single atrocity of the troubles. I rushed into work that
Saturday afternoon to help out and was quickly going live on our
Sports Results programme, of all things, reporting on indications
that the death toll would be high. I never thought it would soar
to twenty-nine, with three hundred people injured. I compiled a
series of reports that night from pictures which were being fed
through UTV. It was my colleague, Jane Loughrey, who valiantly
and magnificently captured the real horror of the tragedy when
she visited the scene and the hell that was the local hospital. The
following day, I voiced-over the heart-breaking images from
amateur video footage of the Saturday afternoon devastation.
They are reports I have never watched again.

I was delighted to get away from Northern Ireland the next
week for a break with Emma and my ex-wife Joan in Barcelona.
However, I wasn't able to leave Omagh behind. On several
occasions, people from home stopped me in the street or on buses
to ask me exactly what had happened because they hadn't heard
much detail. One couple kept me talking for so long that I had to
abandon plans to visit Barcelona's Nou Camp stadium. I didn't

really mind as the information appeared to help them come to terms with the horror.

The fact that the bomb killed an equal number of Protestants and Catholics united the province as never before. More than likely this prevented loyalists from attempting to avenge Omagh. Yet loyalist dissidents were starting to make noises in the background. Within a few months they were emerging from the shadows and I got the call to meet them.

It was November 1998 when I took the first phone call from a man who said that he and some colleagues wanted to meet me to discuss new loyalist thinking. He wouldn't give me any names, but instructed me to drive to the roundabout at Nutt's Corner, near Moira, and park my car there at a precise time. They would take it from there. I was to be alone, without a cameraman, but the man told me to bring a stills camera. As I say, I had no idea who this man was, so it was with some trepidation that I kept this particular appointment. No sooner had I stopped my car, than another vehicle raced in behind me, parking in such a way that it would have been impossible for me to see a number plate, even if I had wanted to. I was motioned into the back seat of this car and ordered not to look at the occupants. It was too dark to see them anyway. Shortly after we set off, the man in the backseat beside me apologised saying he would have to put a hood over my head. For the next forty-five minutes I was driven round the highways and byways of County Antrim, before being told we had arrived at our destination.

A group of men led me into a hall of some sort and removed the hood. Blinking into the light, I saw I was sharing a room with eight hooded and masked men, all fully armed. A man, described as the terrorists' chaplain, opened the proceedings with a reading from the Bible. Despite my unease at the situation, I wanted to laugh at the sight of the heavily armed men with their heads lowered in prayerful repose. Then two of the men kept guard at the door as the other six posed for me to take a picture. I noted handguns, rifles, a submachine-gun, a sawn-off shotgun and Russian-made grenades on the table in front of them. One of the men read a statement. They were calling themselves the Orange Volunteers and they didn't believe the IRA's war was over. They threatened to take action against individual Provos, who had been freed from jail under the Good Friday Agreement. I was allowed to ask some questions before our meeting was concluded with another prayer session. I half expected them to thrust a collection plate in my face.

The hood was placed back over my head and I was returned to my car. There had been virtually no conversation in the car, except when I asked the big bloke beside me what would have happened if we had been stopped by the police. How on earth, I wondered, would they have explained my hooded presence in the back seat? "Don't worry, we had scout cars all over the place," he replied.

The police questioned me for hours about my experience, demanding the tiniest detail. They wanted to know if I was aware of crossing gravel or a pavement. I soon understood that they hoped to link the Orange Volunteers' stunt with the arrest in Belfast that same night of a dissident loyalist. But they couldn't make any connection. The Orange Volunteers carried out a number of terrorist attacks, mainly low-key, and after a series of arrests, they vanished from the scene as quickly as they had come onto it.

That wasn't the last of my unusual contacts with dissident loyalists, however. After receiving yet another phone call from yet another unknown man, I went to one of County Antrim's top hotels and was ushered into a room where twelve men were gathered around a table. They told me they were the Ulster Protestant Movement for Justice (UPMJ) and said they were firmly opposed to the Good Friday Agreement. One of their members read out a statement which, like the Orange Volunteers, included chunks of New Testament scripture. They denied they were paramilitaries. At first, the group didn't want to put forward a spokesman to be interviewed. Then former Ulster Democratic Party (UDP) member, Harry Speers, reluctantly agreed to talk to me.

He said, "We are opposed to violence but we can understand it because we have seen what it has achieved for others. However, we are not going down that road. We want to take Gandhi as our example. We know we will be called bigots and crackpots but we are not a crowd of lunatics quoting from the Old Testament." Speers said the UPMJ would soon reveal what actions they would be taking to underline their message.

Speers' actions were to brutally contradict his words. One day, short of a month later, Speers and a teenager kicked a harmless Protestant man, Trevor Lowry, to death at Glengormley in the mistaken belief that he was a Catholic. I sat in court as Speers was subsequently jailed for life for the murder. In my report, I replayed his "Gandhi" speech so that everyone could see and hear what hypocrisy looked and sounded like.

CHAPTER 11

Twin Terrors

The world isn't exactly your oyster in Ulster. Well, not in Ulster Television at any rate. When you work as a reporter for a comparatively small regional company like UTV your ambitions tend to be tailored to the limitations of the news beat you cover. So, you don't really expect to report on some of the world's biggest stories – yet the dawn of a new millennium saw me reporting on two of the most horrendous tragedies ever to occur anywhere on the globe – the 9/11 bombing and the Asian tsunami.

Like everyone else on the planet, I will never forget where I was when I heard about the horror of the Twin Towers. I was in the dry cleaner's shop collecting a suit when the radio announced the first strike. I dashed home, just over a mile away, in time to catch the second attack unfolding on my television screen, little thinking that within a week I would be in New York myself. The day after the plane bombings my boss, Rob Morrison, rang to say that UTV wanted me to go to America to produce news reports and a half-hour special for the *Insight* current affairs programme.

It took several days to finalise the arrangements. For a start, the American government had banned flights in and out of the country. Just as it looked like we might have to cancel the trip, we received confirmation that we would be going on the first Aer Lingus flight from Ireland into New York. The atmosphere at Belfast International Airport was tense. Ground staff were asking all passengers if they would give up their seats to anxious Americans who wanted to get home to their families. Things were even worse at Shannon airport during our stop-over. Hundreds of American soldiers, who were flying into the unknown, wandered the complex in a daze. One serviceman in front of me in a shop queue had a little Irish sew-on badge in his hand. "It just might be my last souvenir of anywhere," he said to the assistant.

Our UTV party consisted of cameraman Brian McVeigh, a freelance from Tyrone and my producer Mary Curry. We tried to talk ourselves into an upbeat mood but once we were in the air a general sense of nervousness was palpable. None of us on that plane really knew what we were flying into. A pretty stewardess told me that she and her colleagues had volunteered to man our flight; their bosses weren't going to force anyone to work on this one. When we landed, I did something that normally makes me wince on long flights – I joined in the cheering and applause for the pilots and crew. I've never been so relieved to have safely arrived at a destination.

The taxi ride to our Manhattan hotel was an equally eerie journey. The smoke was still billowing from the famous skyline and you didn't need to be told that there was something missing. Though mentally and physically exhausted, Brian and Mary both agreed to my request for us all to have just a couple of hours sleep. At 5.00am we headed downtown towards Ground Zero to start work. The closest we could get was Canal Street, a few blocks from the carnage. It was close enough. You sensed death everywhere. Even at dawn, the streets were filled with hollow-eyed rescuers walking to and from the heart of the disaster, while a convoy of huge trucks hauled massive girders away from the scene. The first person I interviewed was fireman Timothy O'Toole, an Irish-American, whose face was caked with grime as he told me, "My brothers are dying in there. It's horrible. I am hoping that people in there are going to be alright but, as the days go on, it's getting worse and worse. I am not the same person I was just a few days ago. I have turned to God. I am praying to God every day." Another rescuer, Frank Segarra, said, "It's still smoking in there at the bottom and then, suddenly, a thirty-foot flame will just jump up. For anybody to come out of there alive would be a miracle from God." That morning Mayor Rudy Guilliani had urged people to return to work and by first light office workers were pouring up from the subways, determined to show the terrorists they wouldn't be defeated. "Have you ever seen a spirit like this?" one woman asked me. Yes, I thought, dozens of times after terrorist outrages – albeit on a smaller scale – back home.

What really got to me was the incessant stream of distraught people, holding up photographs of their missing relatives in front of our camera, pleading with us to show them on air. I gave up telling them the chances of anyone in Ireland being able to help them were nil. I was proved wrong just a few hours later. After sending a five minute package back to Belfast, we went to St Patrick's Cathedral to cover a memorial service for members of the emergency services. As the fire officers and police emerged from the church, thousands of people on the pavements cheered and clapped them. I interviewed a couple of fire-fighters and one of them told me his son, Mickey Kirby, was missing along with a friend called Brian Monaghan. It transpired that Brian Monaghan had strong family links with Belfast and his relatives were shocked to hear about him on the local news. Mickey and Brian were both later confirmed dead.

The small world syndrome was reconfirmed for me when a bloke standing beside me on Fifth Avenue said, "Phenomenon".

He told me he was Dee McKeown from Finaghy, and he was a neighbour of a friend of mine. We also interviewed Belfast-born restaurant owner, Eugene Devlin, and his friend Ronan Downs. Their business was just a few blocks from the World Trade Centre and they had lost countless customers. They had to lock survivors inside their premises as the dust from the collapse of the Towers engulfed the entire area. A chef from Warrenpoint described how fear gripped everyone as rumours circulated that five more planes were on their way to attack New York.

There's also the story of Roger Smyth, a paramedic from the Antrim Road area of Belfast. When Roger saw the horrific events unfold from his Brooklyn home across the river, he bravely drove into the danger zone to tend to the dying and the injured at a makeshift medical point near the Twin Towers. A keen photographer, he also took a remarkable picture of fire officers defiantly hoisting the Stars and Stripes flag on top of the rubble, a photo which hangs proudly on the wall of my home. What was particularly chilling was Roger's emergency services badge number, 9110. The only way you could read it was 9/11 at ground zero. Roger's selfless heroism was rewarded by the American authorities. They didn't award him any medals; instead they allowed him to stay in New York despite his not having the proper papers.

The scale of the tragedy in New York was almost impossible to comprehend, as was the jarring silence of this usually terrifically noisy city. No horns blared in the traffic jams. No taxi drivers screamed or swore. One cabbie told us he didn't know how to respond when other drivers waved him on in front of them into their lanes. All over the city something was stirring – patriotic fervour. Flag-makers simply couldn't produce enough Stars and Stripes to meet the demand. People dealt with the disaster in whatever way they could. Some travelled hundreds of miles to man soup kitchens near hospitals close to Ground Zero. Others went to look at the tributes to the victims in parks like Union Square, which had been turned into memorial gardens, carpeted with flowers, teddy bears and photographs of the dead. At the time, it was thought that up to six thousand people had been killed. The real figure has, thankfully, turned out to be much less than that. Still, three thousand lives were wiped out in the blink of an eye and for what? The hunger for revenge was everywhere. Newspapers carried Osama Bin Laden's photograph in "Wanted: Dead or Alive" posters on their front pages. The inside pages were full of individual tragedies, including how the bombings were threatening to cripple Broadway. Naturally enough, people were too distracted to go to see make-believe drama in theatres, and one of the shows which had to close was from back home.

Stones in His Pockets by Marie Jones had been a particular favourite of mine and I had championed the play on UTV for years, from its first run at the West Belfast Festival to its glittering opening night in the West End of London. Now here was the same show in New York and it, unfortunately, was about to close. We went round to the theatre, just off Times Square, to film patrons leaving one of the last performances.

Again I experienced the small world syndrome. As I stood with Brian the cameraman, a woman walked up to me and asked me, with a strong South Down accent, if I was Siofra O'Reilly's partner. She said she knew her dad, a retired GP, in Newry and as we chatted she pointed out a relative who had been with her at the play; he had had a narrow escape in the disaster. So I thrust my microphone under Niall Feeley's nose and he told me his story. Afterwards I went to the stage door and sought out the play's stars Conleth Hill and Sean Campion. I asked the lads to talk about their experiences, but Conleth didn't want to do it and the reason for his reluctance made me even more depressed. Conleth's father, Patsy, was a marvel of a man, a BBC cameraman, and a veteran of the troubles. Even though he worked for "the other side", I loved Patsy's company, his anecdotes and his jokes. Conleth explained that Patsy was close to death back home in Ballycastle and he simply couldn't bring himself to put on a show for an interview. It was completely understandable. So Sean did the chat and spoke eloquently of how the shutting down of a play paled into insignificance when compared to what was happening on the streets of New York.

Mary and Brian had never seen the play so we decided to take the next night off to see *Stones*. It was a nightmare of a night, though not through any fault of the play or players. The first half was its usual hilarious self and, at the interval, we went next door to a bar for a swift drink. We arrived just as President George Bush was starting his televised address to the nation and the bar went quiet. Bush was, basically, declaring war. He scared the crap out of Mary, Brian and myself. We dragged ourselves back into the theatre for the second half but I don't think we managed a laugh between us. We wanted to get out of there, out of New York, out of America, and go home.

However, before we could leave we wanted to film right in the heart of the Ground Zero, a sight I will not forget. I remember thinking that I would never see anything worse than this. Within a few years, I would be proved wrong by the destruction left in the wake of the tsunami.

Unlike 9/11, where the scale of the crisis was quickly apparent, it took several days to appreciate just how catastrophic the tsunami on Boxing Day 2004 had been. I first heard about the killer wave on an early morning news bulletin on Radio Ulster. They reported that a Northern Ireland man had survived a huge wave in Thailand. Only later did they mention the possibility that many people had been killed. Their news values sharpened as the day wore on and they reversed the two strands of the story to tell us firstly how hundreds of people had been killed before referring to the local survivor.

As it became clear that tens of thousands of people had perished, an old *Portadown Times* colleague, David Gough, who helped run the Concern charity in Ireland, contacted me to see if I wanted to go with his organisation to one of the worst hit areas in Sri Lanka. Then I heard that a Cookstown man was missing on Phi Phi island, off Thailand, and his relatives were planning to go to Asia in a bid to find him. Contact was made with Connor Keightley's family and they said they would have no problems with my accompanying them to file reports on their visit. They even organised the flight arrangements through a relative who was involved in the travel business.

So, on January 4, 2005, at Belfast City Airport, I met with Connor's sisters, Michelle and Darina, his uncle Damian Coyle, and his cousin Gavin O'Neill, for what would be a most intensely emotional and difficult assignment for me and my cameraman, the larger-than-life Albert Kirk. For the next seven days, we lived and breathed the family's dreams and despairs. We watched as their slender hopes were raised after Michelle spotted a photograph on a hospital notice-board of an injured survivor who looked remarkably like Connor, only to see them dashed half-an-hour later when the authorities told them the man in the picture was Swedish. We travelled to a ruined Phi Phi. It had been totally torn apart by two tsunamis that smashed together on the tiny island resort, killing hundreds and hundreds of tourists and locals. Truth to tell, Albert and I had never shared the sisters' optimism that Connor could be found alive. Three hours on Phi Phi ended any lingering illusions for us. The place was completely decimated and there was a poignant moment on a beautiful beach as the Keightley family stood side by side in a reflective tribute to Connor. Damian and Gavin left Darina and Michelle with their own thoughts and the girls clung to one another. It was a scene which would have melted the hardest heart. The sisters then collected shells from the ravaged beach to give to their relatives as mementoes of Connor.

After Phi Phi, Albert and I visited another tsunami disaster zone in Thailand, several hours north of our base at Phuket. What we found was far worse that we expected. The entire coastal region looked as if a nuclear bomb had levelled it. I sat on a beach at Koah Lak and tried to imagine what it must have been like to have been sunbathing in such a serene spot only days earlier when the tidal wave struck. From watching amateur video pictures on television, I had thought it would have been possible to outrun the tsunami. But sitting there, I knew it would have been impossible to get away. It had flattened everything in its path for two or three miles inland. We even discovered a police patrol boat lying in a field several miles away from the ocean. Nearby, Thai people watched as a search went on for cars that had been swept off the main road into a lagoon – and this was two miles from the sea.

We filmed in several makeshift mortuaries in temples along the coast. We saw hundreds of coffins, countless bodies and most appalling of all for me, scores of pictures of bloated bodies on what were called the "walls of death" outside the morgues. Dozens of them were babies. How anyone could have recognized any of the bodies was beyond me. The stench of death was sickening. In the morgues we witnessed the all-too-familiar grief as relatives were told that their loved ones had been positively identified. Afterwards, it felt almost immoral for us to return to our luxury hotel, the Hilton Arcadia resort in Phuket. It's the biggest hotel in Thailand and had escaped unscathed. The opulence was staggering, yet neither Albert nor I were able to partake of the spa, the pools or its other five star pampering. Our only relaxation,

after a day's filming and a night's editing, was a couple of late
night beers and the odd after-midnight room service meal on our
balcony. The hotel put on entertainment every night but neither
the performers nor the few guests – mainly forensic teams from
around the world – could muster any enthusiasm. Listening to a
girl band singing Abba songs just a few miles from where
hundreds of bodies lay unidentified felt utterly wrong.

Albert and I had time for only one real meal during our time
in Phuket, in a restaurant not far from the hotel. The place was
deserted and we later ended up in a street which was packed with
mostly empty bars. It didn't dawn on us immediately that these
bars were the sort of places for which Thailand is infamous, where
visiting men are more interested in leers than beers and getting
frisky instead of whiskey. I don't expect anyone to believe me, but
Albert and I really did spend our short time in the bars playing
Connect Four with a couple of the locals. The locals told us the
tsunami had wrecked the tourist trade, including *that* side of the
tourist trade.

After our night off, we re-joined the Keightleys in the town of
Krabi, where they had been staying for the last couple of days. The
Irish Foreign Minister, Dermot Ahern, was on a fact-finding
mission, and he met the Keightleys at their hotel. He assured
them his staff and a team of visiting Garda Siochana forensic
experts would do everything they could for them. It was the eve
of the Keightleys' return to Ireland. Albert and I offered the family
a lift from their base in Krabi to Phuket in the minibus we had
hired. The mood was downcast and it was obvious from Damian's
demeanour that we were on the brink of a breakthrough, though
he didn't say anything. As we travelled through what in ordinary
circumstances would have been the most breathtaking scenery,
Damian took a phone call from the Irish Embassy, asking him and
the family to divert to the Pearl Hotel in downtown Phuket,

where the ambassador Dan Mulhall was waiting. No one spoke. For the first time during the entire trip, I asked Albert to put the camera down. The sound of the sisters' anguish confirmed that they had received the worst news: Connor's body had been found and positively identified. For Albert and I, it was like losing one of our own and emotion overtook the both of us. As the family emerged from their private meeting, the Embassy staff offered them their own transport back to their hotel in Phuket to allow them to grieve on their own. But Darina and Michelle said they wanted to travel back with Albert and me. They explained that we had been with them from the start and they wanted us to be with them at the finish; that they had come to Thailand as a family of four and were returning to Ireland as a family of six. That night in our hotel in Phuket, after Albert and I had finished our edit and sent our package back to Belfast, we joined the family to wake Connor in a way I'm sure he would have been proud of.

On our return to Belfast, Albert and I immediately set about producing a thirty-minute documentary about the Keightleys' journey to find their brother, and how their sadness at the end of it was tempered with relief at finding his body. In the documentary we were able to go into greater depth about how the body had been discovered and identified. The Keightleys had studied lists containing descriptions of hundreds and hundreds of bodies that had been ferried to the town of Krabi from Phi Phi. They were able to quickly eliminate many of the bodies from their deliberations, though several caught their attention because they were similar in height to Connor. One corpse in particular – number 467 – was wearing a Storm watch like the one Connor wore. The Garda forensic team carried out detailed examinations of the body, matching dental records and photographs of a tattoo on Connor's back. Eventually, they were able to declare that this was definitely Connor.

I am pleased to say that our relationship with the Keightley family hasn't ended. I was honoured to have them as guests for a performance of *The History of the Troubles* at the Grand Opera House, and they have entertained Albert and I in their hometown of Cookstown, when they presented the two of us with shells from the beach in Phi Phi where the family held their vigil for Connor.

CHAPTER 12

Collared by the Big Man

Reporters, as the name suggests, are supposed to report on the news. Not make it. However that old maxim was turned on its head when the Rev Ian Paisley grabbed me by the lapels during a live television interview, catapulting me onto countless front pages right around the world. It was November 2003 and I was interviewing him at the count for the Assembly elections in the Joey Dunlop Leisure Centre in Ballymoney. The DUP leader was, as usual, a racing certainty to take the chequered flag in the election. There was a lot of speculation about his health and about whether or not his party would oust the Ulster Unionists as the biggest pro-Union grouping. He had said little or nothing in the run-up to the election and the big man didn't seem quite so big on that crisp winter's day. He appeared frail and gaunt, and was wrapped and hatted up against the cold.

Among the media in Ballymoney the race was on to be the one to get Ian Paisley to do his first live interview in ages. Naturally I was determined I was going to win, and beat the BBC who were constantly saying how much it meant to them to get *the* big interviews with the winning politicians. I had been given the nod that Paisley would talk to me first after his victory had been declared. However, I wasn't taking any chances. I was waiting to pounce and I quickly led him over to UTV's live position in the tiny little area where the press gathered. So keen were our people back at base to get him that they shouted in my earpiece to start the interview immediately.

After the usual formalities, I started to press him more and more about whether or not he would speak to Sinn Féin. He was clearly getting tired of the question. Suddenly he stretched out his arms and grabbed hold of the lapels of my favourite blue suit and bellowed, "No! Do I need to repeat it? Do I need to take you by the neck and say no, I'm not? I am not talking to Sinn Féin. And anybody that talks to Sinn Féin will be out of my party."

In bewilderment, my first reaction was a dazed smile but as he continued to rant, I regained my composure. A thousand thoughts flooded my mind. Should I forcibly remove his hands? Should I tell him I was stopping the interview? Or should I just tell him where to get off? I wondered what my cameraman was doing. I prayed he hadn't stayed on a single shot of Paisley and instead had pulled out to a two-shot to show this surreal confrontation. Then I remembered my cameraman was a slick operator called Brian Newman, who was on top of the game. I also thought that this was fantastic television and hoped it was still going out live on air. It was. Afterwards, I turned my phone back on and it rang non-stop. Journalists from other newspapers were calling to see if what they had heard had really happened. Luckily, a photographer, who had been covering the election count for the Press Association, came over to me and said he had caught the lot on camera. He even let me help him pick the best shot for distribution.

I actually get on quite well with Ian Paisley and, later in the leisure centre canteen, he joked that he hoped he hadn't hurt me. Matching his mood, I said that if he had I would have decked him. I also told him he had ruined my favourite suit. "Send the bill to the DUP," he replied.

Naturally enough, UTV reran the incident over and over again. The next morning, I was back in Ballymoney, which was now packed with Sinn Féin supporters, eager to see their candidate Philip McGuigan make history by winning a seat in Ian Paisley's backyard. I knew many of the Sinn Féin supporters from regular visits to Ballycastle and they kept telling me that I should sue Paisley for assault. "He put his hands on you, that is assault," said one man. "You could make a fortune." I didn't take their advice. I knew Paisley had been making a serious point when he grabbed me. What he was saying at the time became the most important DUP utterance of the elections. Equally, I knew he was not trying to hurt me – otherwise, I would indeed have cut up rough with him.

Meanwhile the event became quite a talking point at home and abroad. I started to receive e-mails from all over the world, including Australia and Canada. My brother Norman even rang from Toronto to inquire if I was okay. I couldn't understand the fuss until more e-mails arrived from Canada, where one publication had reported that Ian Paisley had assaulted me, causing me actual bodily harm. It got so bad that Suzanne Breen, of the *News Letter*, even ran a story on the Little-Paisley confrontation. She tried to play the whole thing down and sought my reaction. I agreed with her line that it was a storm in a teacup. The fact that Paisley and I are about the same height obviously contributed to his actions. I must be about the only reporter in Ireland whose lapels he could grab without having to bend down. Seriously though, I was pleased with the fact I didn't shrink from Paisley during the interview, even after he went for my jugular. I was delighted to read in the *Andersonstown News* a few days later, television critic, Concubhar O Liathain, describing me as a hero for standing firm to the big man. "Some day the city fathers and mothers will knock down those old statues celebrating the colonial heroes around City Hall and a monument to a real act of journalistic courage will occupy the empty plinth," he wrote.

The press made a big thing of the Big Man and the Little reporter; for weeks I couldn't go out the door without someone referring to Ballymoney. Politicians like Gerry Kelly of Sinn Féin and David Trimble of the Ulster Unionists made a big play of singling me out in the media scrum to grab me by the collar. I even had to stay away from pubs for a while because so many people, with a few pints in them, started to think they were comedians, literally queuing up to take hold of my lapels. It was funny the first couple of times, but the joke quickly wore thin along with the material in my jacket. And I won't forget going to the Odyssey Arena in Belfast to see Fleetwood Mac in concert. As I was searching for our seats, someone lunged towards me. They missed my jacket collar and instead caught my shirt. I heard the rip of cotton with buttons flying everywhere. I was bloody fuming and fully intended to punch the nutter on the jaw. Then I recognised my attacker to be my oul mate Gary Honeyford from Sky Television! He was totally shocked and kept muttering mortified apologies, but standing there with my exposed hairless chest and ample stomach I wasn't exactly in the mood to accept them. I covered myself with my leather jacket and headed to my seat, surrounded by thousands of people who had taken their jackets off because the arena was so hot. Gary, it must be said, later bought me a lovely new shirt to make amends!

My encounter with Paisley in Ballymoney also ended up in a couple of books. Dean Godson included the picture in his biography of Ulster Unionist leader David Trimble, and the photograph was also included on the cover of the 2004 *Northern Ireland Yearbook*. Five or six months later, I was a bit surprised, to say the least, to hear Ian Paisley's account of the incident when he addressed his party's annual conference. Firstly he claimed I had asked him repeatedly if he would talk with IRA/Sinn Féin. This was not a phrase I have ever, or would ever, use. It was Sinn Féin, plain and simple. He described for his adoring audience how he had caught this large reporter by the lapels: "In fact I nearly choked him and told him in no uncertain language, never. And never it is." His quote was completely wrong and when I checked the original text of his speech I noticed the "choking" remark wasn't in it. A DUP contact said that the party leader was simply playing to the crowd and over-egged the Ballymoney incident.

There were happier spin-offs from the episode. At UTV's Christmas party in 2004, Mike Nesbitt made a speech in which he looked back over the highs and the lows of the newsroom year. He referred to the envy which he and other political commentators in UTV, like Ken Reid and Fearghal McKinney, felt about the incident. He pointed out that they were the UTV people who did the lion's share of the political interviews, yet the very person who disliked having to cover anything to do with politics had managed to get *the* image and *the* quote of the year. Mike then presented me with a massive blow-up block-mounted poster of *the* picture – a photograph that hung in our guestroom at home until one guest took it down and stashed it behind a wardrobe. She complained that she couldn't sleep in the same room as the picture. But she wouldn't say which of the big men bothered her the most.

My face to face with Paisley isn't the only encounter with a politician that has been recorded for posterity. In 1992 UTV commisioned the artist Flora McDonnell to produce a series of paintings reflecting the working life of the station. That April, Flora accompanied a crew and myself when we went to the Springfield Road in west Belfast to cover the murder of Catholic woman Philomena Hanna by the UFF. Philomena had been a chemist's shop assistant and a gunman had simply walked in and shot her. The twenty-six year old mother of two regularly crossed the peaceline to deliver prescriptions to loyalist areas of the city.

One of the people I interviewed about the murder was Sinn Féin president Gerry Adams. Flora later recreated the interview on canvas. The painting is now part of the UTV art collection and hangs on the walls of Havelock House when it is not part of a touring exhibition around Ireland. "Ivan Little interviewing Gerry Adams, 1992" is one of around fifty paintings featured in a UTV book about the art collection. I hope to acquire a print of it one day for my own collection and it may have an interesting companion.

For an artist of my acquaintance has told me he is currently working on a painting of my encounter with Ian Paisley. I reckon the two works together would make for interesting viewing. Just imagine hanging Ian Paisley and Gerry Adams in the same room...

CHAPTER 13

The Boss, Bestie and Bobby Dylan

There's no point denying it, I have a lot more than just a little of the star-struck old fool in me. I am in my element when I come face-to-face with a celebrity, especially from the world of entertainment. And this journalism caper, even in a comparative backwater like Belfast, has thrown plenty of opportunities my way: Billy Connolly, Kenneth Branagh, Diana Rigg, Andrew Lloyd-Webber, Diana Ross, and even Bob Dylan. I've met them all. Nothing, however, will equal the euphoria I felt as I stood on the stage of the King's Hall in Belfast, interviewing the "Boss". Bruce Springsteen was, is and always will be my rock and roll Messiah. I had seen him perform in Slane, in Wembley and twice at the RDS in Dublin. Then the chance to meet him landed on my lap in March 1996. His record company representative in Ireland, Brian Jordan, rang to ask me if I fancied being one of only two Irish journalists to interview him during his visits to Dublin and Belfast. Did I what?

As with so many megastars, word was that Springsteen was difficult, his flunkeys were difficult and his management were difficult. I was nervous enough as it was. Thankfully the reality of the experience was completely different, the Boss and his minions couldn't have been any *less* difficult. I turned up with my crew long before the appointed hour and we were invited into the King's Hall arena for the sound-check. Unbelievably, we were able to stay for all of it, as Bruce readied himself for the gig. I got talking to his co-manager, Barbara Carr, and she turned out to be a real diamond. She wanted to know all there was to know about living in Belfast and I tried, as best I could, to give her the lowdown. During the conversation, I asked her if Bruce would give me his autograph at the end of the interview. She seemed surprised and said no one had ever sought permission before. She assured me she would have a word with the Boss. Springsteen indicated he was ready to start the interview, which I had been told would be restricted to just two questions. However, that's not the way it turned out. He spoke for about six or seven minutes, discussing his solo acoustic tour, his visits to the Shankill and the Falls earlier that day, and his knowledge of Irish traditional music. At one point, he even prefaced an answer with the words, "That's a good question." Wow, the Boss thought I had asked a good question! I was walking on air. And yes, he did give me his autograph, even remembering that my name was Ivan.

Another "big name" interview also came my way, via Brian Jordan. This time it was American diva, Mariah Carey. She was in Dublin in March 1999 and was granting an audience to a handful of hacks, myself included. Her reputation as a demanding pain-in-the-arse had preceded her and there were all sorts of conditions laid down by her American management before we were allowed to go ahead with the interview. Mariah had an army of fifteen aides at her beck and call: make-up artists, hair stylists, clothes coordinators and even a lighting technician who set up his own rig before checking our camera to make sure it would show his boss in the best possible light. All this, of course, made me wonder what the star of the show would be like. I had heard all the rumours about the hissy fits, her arrogance and her rudeness. However, I am glad to say that she was completely laid back. As we waited for her beauticians to beautify her and her pamperers to pamper her, she chatted away to me, telling me the main reason for her visit to Ireland was that her mother was trying to find her Irish roots in Kerry. Their only problem, she said, was that even in the wilds of the west of Ireland, the newspaper photographers had managed to find her and she couldn't understand how they tracked her down. I asked her if the stretch limos, which were sitting outside the hotel in Dublin, were her mode of transport in Kerry. When she answered yes, I suggested that the limos could have been the clue, because you don't see too many stretches trundling around the Kingdom. God bless her, she seemed genuinely surprised. When the camera started to turn, she was warm and friendly. She even agreed to pose for a picture with me – at Brian Jordan's suggestion I hasten to add – and we were also invited to hang around for a drink with her and her Mum!

Kylie Minogue was another star who turned out to be a lot more co-operative than the begrudgers had predicted. I only went to Belfast International Airport to record her arriving before a concert in April 1990 because Emma was a Kylie fanatic and *she* wanted to see her close-up. Kylie's burly minders had other ideas and tried to push the tiny singer past the handful of journalists and fans until she put her size three foot down and shouted to them, "No, let them do their interviews." Despite having little or no make-up on, she wasn't afraid of the cameras. I later interviewed a couple of fans and the daughter of my former *Telegraph* colleague, Eddie McIlwaine, came out with the immortal line, "I didn't think she would have had spots."

Another interview I recorded at the airport was with Bono, the lead singer of U2, on his arrival for a 1986 gig at the King's Hall. Again, I had been warned to expect a hostile reaction but Bono was only too happy to talk. My interview with him has ended up in scores of homes in Canada, where my U2-crazy niece, Sandra, ran off countless "bootleg" copies of the encounter between "my uncle and Bono". I also received a request for a copy of my six-minute report on the concert itself from U2's management, who later sent a thank-you note, saying the band loved the coverage.

One man who *did* live up to his reputation for weirdness was Bob Dylan. He has provided me with one of the funniest "celeb" packages of my UTV career. We got a tip-off about which flight he would be coming in on, before his concert at the Maysfield Leisure Centre in February 1993. One or two fans had also discovered the details and were there to meet him too. However, Dylan refused to sign autographs or even acknowledge his fans and, unsurprisingly, also refused to say anything to the likes of us. What *was* surprising was his refusal to step into his waiting car while my cameraman, Marty Gibson, was filming him. To this day, I have no idea who was in the car or why Dylan didn't want to get in it. He hung about the airport exit for at least thirty minutes, reading every advertisement in the place, every notice board. He never actually complained about what Marty was doing. A promoter, eventually, asked Marty to stop filming and once the camera was switched off, Dylan jumped into a taxi and away he went. Rumours were rife that Dylan had a lady friend in Belfast and he didn't want her or her car to be identified, but I never could find real evidence for this.

Ironically, Dylan's old backing group, The Band, were to be my biggest "celeb" disappointment. I was, and still am, obsessed with The Band and have collected every album, every book, and every newspaper article about them. In the 1980s in Toronto, I got to see a solo concert by my hero, Levon Helm, The Band's drummer and, in my humble opinion, one of the finest voices in rock and roll. The gig, in a tiny, sweaty club on Yonge Street, was one of the best I have ever attended. Still, I had never seen The Band until they came to Dublin in June 1996 as part of a reunion tour. The support act, as good luck would have it, were Four Men and a Dog, a traditional Irish music band whose members were mostly from the north. I had got drunk a few times with the Dogs after compiling a series of reports on them for UTV and, in later years, they had been become friendly with The Band. They had also recorded an album in Levon Helm's studio in Woodstock and I thought the tie-up a perfect excuse to cover The Band's trip to Dublin for a UTV feature. So I got tickets for the two shows they were doing on successive nights, planning to work the first night and simply enjoy the second gig. The Dogs told The Band's manager about my devotion to their cause and he gave me permission to film as much of the concert at the Olympia as I wanted. But things didn't go according to plan.

After we had filmed The Band coming on stage, I met up with the Dogs for a quick chat. When I returned to my seat, Siofra told me that something was wrong; Levon Helm had fallen off his drum stool and had thrown away his cherished mandolin. Then I noticed the bass player, Rick Danko, looked somewhat unsteady on his feet. Mid-way through the set he walked off stage, never to return. The manager came sprinting through the theatre to tell us to stop filming. He didn't give a reason but it was clear that some of The Band were, shall we say, tired and emotional. This was followed by Levon Helm telling the Irish audience, "It's great to be here in LONDON." Fifty minutes after taking the stage, The Band or what was left of them took themselves off it. End of show. Dozens of fans besieged the box office, demanding their money back. I had to forget my own disappointment as a fan and interview the dissenters for what would be a negative and critical story for UTV. I was so deflated that I couldn't bring myself to stay on in Dublin for the second night's gig and returned to

Belfast in a huff. My despondency was only compounded by later reports that the second concert had been a real winner, with The Band back on the top of their form. It later emerged that some of the musicians, renowned for the hard living of their younger days on the road, had succumbed to the temptation of something or other in London and they obviously hadn't quite got it out of their systems by the time they reached Dublin. The Dogs had assured me, before the gig, that they would persuade Levon Helm to do an interview with me. But it never happened. It was the one that got away.

Another musician well known for his excesses was Phil Lynott. I was thrilled to meet him after a Thin Lizzy gig at the Ulster Hall and couldn't believe his antics, or his stamina, at a drinks party in the Europa Hotel. Every time a girl approached him for an autograph, he went into the same routine, asking them if they would like a Lizzy teeshirt as well. Naturally, nobody said no whereupon Phil would suddenly remember that the teeshirts were in his room. One after another, the girls trooped up the stairs, and I presume some of them got more than a teeshirt for their trouble.

As well as rock stars, my job has given me the chance to interview famous sporting greats and there were few bigger than the soccer legend, Sir Stanley Matthews. I was lucky enough to meet him in the mid 90s. I went to Westminster to film a piece about a new soccer book published by MPs in a project organised by one Alistair Campbell, who was later to become Tony Blair's spin doctor. Sir Stanley was everything I imagined he would be: shy, modest and quietly spoken. Just as another hero of mine, Denis Law, was quite the opposite: cocky, confident and hilariously funny. Denis had come to Belfast as a surprise guest at the official ceremony to grant his Old Trafford buddy, George Best, the freedom of Castlereagh, where he was born. For me, the visit to Burren Way was a trip down memory lane because my father used to deliver milk to a house three doors down from the Best home and I used to dream that I would see Bestie on his one of his return visits. Once, and only once, did I see him coming out of the house, looking every inch the genius he was. Not quite the same look of the man I was to meet in later years, though I must say I enjoyed getting hammered with him one afternoon in his Chelsea drinking haunt, the Phene Arms, after recording an interview in the pub's beer garden about plans to make a movie about him.

However, I felt totally ashamed of myself and my profession in 2001 when I was sent to doorstep Best at his former home in Portavogie amid reports that he had gone back on the drink after a life-saving liver transplant operation. Neighbours shouted insults at us as we stood on the road outside his house. For once, I agreed with them and thought we should leave the poor guy alone. After an hour's stake-out I cleared off, taking my memories of a magnificent footballer with me.

One of George's former Man United team-mates, Sir Bobby Charlton, was a major disappointment for me. I had gone to Lancashire to report on Northern Irish kids taking part in his summer soccer school. The interview with Sir Bobby was boring and bland and it was clear he couldn't wait for it to end, little realising that I shared his feelings completely.

Another famous interviewee I didn't warm to was actor Alan Rickman. He played the Sheriff of Nottingham in the film, *Robin Hood, Prince of Thieves*. I was in London covering a youth drama event at the National Theatre and the organisers agreed to my request for an interview with one of the patrons, Diana Rigg. She was lovely and took time to inquire about my daughter Emma after someone mentioned she was at drama school in London. Then Rickman suddenly appeared out of nowhere for an interview, at the behest of the sponsors. He couldn't have been more unfriendly as he brushed off my questions with disdain. After his and my agony ended, I made it patently clear to him that I hadn't requested the interview and that if he hadn't wanted to do it he should have saved us both the trouble. I wish I had said it with just two words rather than the more civilised mouthful.

Coincidentally, around the same time, back at the Ice Bowl in Dundonald, I interviewed Bryan Adams, the Canadian singer, who had broken all chart records with his theme song from the *Robin Hood* movie, "Everything I do, I do it for you". He was a real gentleman and made a huge fuss of Emma who had come with me on the shoot. He took an eternity to autograph every picture she had brought with her and posed for photograph after photograph. He was the complete opposite of Rickman but perhaps the actor was just having an off night. Anyway, I am not always the best judge of character. Take Gary Glitter, for example. I interviewed him for the *Telegraph* after a concert in Belfast in the 70s and couldn't find enough superlatives to praise him. Look how he turned out.

One woman I had always dreamt of interviewing was the actress Britt Ekland; she was high up on my list of fanciable females. However, when I finally did meet her in 2000, she was a bit of a boke, to use a particularly apt Belfast phrase. She was over here for the Opera House panto and, as always, I went along to the Royal Victoria Hospital for Sick Children to film the cast meeting the young cancer patients. She refused to film an interview with me because she reckoned our lights weren't good enough to do her any justice. My friend, Paddy Jenkins, who was also in the cast, tried to talk her round but the lady was not for turning. Britts out, I thought.

The strangest "celebrity" press conference I ever covered was with the American band, The Eagles, in Dublin in July 1996. They had just reunited for their *Hell Freezes Over* tour. You didn't need to know them to see that these guys were *not* getting back together for the love of the music, or each other. They all arrived separately to the press conference and though they tried to put on a united front, tensions were obvious. It was a bit of a contrast to the last time I had seen The Eagles together, playing support for Procul Harum in Toronto in 1971. In Dublin a quarter of a century later, I groaned when I heard that the one-to-one interview UTV had been granted was with Timothy B. Schmit, who wasn't one of the better known Eagles. Yet, during the interview he gave me a dream of a story when he revealed that his wife wasn't with him in Dublin because she was staying on her aunt's farm – in Dungiven! Schmit said his wife was the daughter of a Northern Irish Catholic mother and a Northern Irish Protestant father. They had emigrated to the east coast of America where she had been born but she was still close to her family in County Derry. This unexpected gem demonstrated the fact that the best stories are often the ones you're not expecting to find.

Like the time in December 1977, when I went to review a gig featuring The Clash at Queen's University. It was the first major punk rock concert in Belfast and I wasn't optimistic about getting a great piece out of it. However, the entertainments officer at Queen's University Students Union, Eamonn McCann, who is now one of Ireland's top promoters, gave me unrestricted backstage access, where there was plenty of action. I watched as Mike Barnett, the manager of The Clash, fought for a bigger fee from McCann and in cash too. He also wanted McCann to fly the band back to England after the concert, to cut out hotel costs. More and more impossible demands were tabled by Barnett and rejected by McCann before the deal was eventually done. Only then did the support act, The Lous, an all-girl punk band from France, burst onto the stage in front of the six hundred fans, who had paid the princely sum of two pounds fifty a head. The Lous roared and swore their way through their frenetic set as the fans did what they had seen English punk fans doing on TV – spitting or gobbing, as they called it – at the musicians. When the girls returned backstage, one of them quickly dropped her hard-as-nails act. As she wiped the spittle off her teeshirt, she realised that it wasn't spittle at all; it was something else which had emanated from another part of a young man's body, a fact that was edited out of my *Telegraph* feature.

As I sat chatting with The Lous, it became apparent that the punk fans outside were getting restless, with no sign of The Clash coming on stage. So off I went in search of an explanation. In a nearby room The Clash were refusing to go stage until their manager got their fee paid out to him in folding money. I don't know about Eamonn McCann but the band and their cash demands were starting to bore the backside off me. Eventually, when they did get on stage, I was pleasantly surprised by their music. I was only twenty-six but felt like Old Father Time standing among the teenagers that made up the crowd. Then I met an old mate who was a bit of a rocker and had slipped into the gig to see what all the fuss was about. One of the last times I had seen him – I'll just call him Denis – was outside Queen's University a few months earlier. The police were then arresting him for drink-driving as ambulance men were taking his equally-inebriated front seat passenger off to hospital, with leg and facial injuries sustained in a car crash. The injuries weren't serious but the passenger was almost murdered by his wife, Joan, when he got home!

Denis, like me, attended all the concerts of any note in Belfast. In the 60s I was lucky enough to see the likes of The Beatles at the King's Hall; Roy Orbison, The Beach Boys and The Rolling Stones at the ABC; and Fleetwood Mac and Jethro Tull at the Ulster Hall. It's hard to believe now, but the tiny Ulster Hall was also the venue for one of the greatest nights in the history of rock and roll in Belfast. That was Friday March 5, 1971 when Led Zeppelin hit town for a memorable concert which also saw the *first-ever* live performance of a song which has become a rock standard, "Stairway to Heaven". I still have my faded ticket for Block B, Row 20 and Seat 9 and it cost me one pound. But, apart from the Zeppelin landing and the old Esoteric Music Society gigs on a Sunday night at Queen's University with guests like The Edgar Broughton Band and Al Stewart, the 70s were a fairly dire time for gigs in Belfast. The troubles scared all but the bravest souls from our battered city.

One man who kept coming back was Rory Gallagher, the Ballyshannon blues guitar hero. He played at least one gig in Belfast every year. I reviewed him a couple of times for the *Melody Maker* magazine and for the *Belfast Telegraph*. I had got the Gallagher bug from Joan. She was a Rory fanatic and had been friendly with the original line-up of Rory's band, Taste, when they played at blues clubs like the Maritime around Belfast. I only interviewed Rory once for the *Telegraph* and I don't know who was more shy, him or me. Luckily, Joan was on hand to help bring Rory and me out of ourselves! Undoubtedly, one of my saddest markings for UTV was to cover Rory's untimely death in 1995. To this day, I have rarely seen a response like it in UTV. The newsroom came to a standstill as people watched the lunchtime report go out. It summed up the esteem with which Rory was held in Belfast. I was asked to produce a half-hour tribute to Gallagher which was broadcast a few weeks after his death, and included interviews with musicians such as Adam Clayton of U2 and Ronnie Drew of The Dubliners. The programme has been repeated several times since and, no matter where I go in Ireland, people still approach me in pubs and restaurants to say thank-you for the documentary – before asking for VHS copies of it!

As well as paying homage to musical legends like Rory, it has also been an enjoyable experience to stumble across the odd newcomer. In 1989, I went to see the band Fairground Attraction at the Grand Opera House. The support singer was an unknown at that time and, when I heard his Belfast accent, I resolved to find out who he was and film an interview with him. The interview kicked off with the question, "Okay, so tell me, who is Brian Kennedy?" It was his first prime-time television broadcast and the rest, as they say, is history. Just six years later, I watched Brian singing with Van Morrison outside Belfast's City Hall. I was doing live inserts that night, during UTV's special programme on the historic visit of President Bill Clinton. He had come to Ireland to endorse the peace process and seventy thousand people gathered in Belfast to see him. His arrival was delayed and UTV kept coming back to me for updates. Thankfully, Van and Brian made the waiting bearable. I got a bit of stick in letters and phone calls when, in one of my links, I joked about not caring that there was still no sign of the President because "who needs Clinton when you've got Kennedy and Morrison?" Some visiting Americans didn't share my Ulster sense of humour.

As well as Brian Kennedy, another man I almost "discovered" for UTV was the Dublin actor, Colin Farrell, now one of the biggest names in Hollywood. Well, actually it was Emma who clocked him, not me. Farrell got his big break in the acting world in 1998 when he was cast in the London run of a play by Belfast writer, Gary Mitchell, one of the few Northern Irish dramatists to write from the loyalist perspective. I went over to London to film a feature for UTV on Gary's play *In a Little World Of Our Own* at the Donmar Warehouse. That night, Emma, who was studying at drama school in London, joined me for the opening night of the play. Afterwards, she gave a rave review – I think for his looks as much as for his acting skills – to one of the cast who had played a young loyalist. Years later we realised it was Colin Farrell. Emma rang to say she had been reading a programme from the play and that Colin Farrell had been *her* man. She also reminded me that I had filmed an excerpt of the play. I rushed off to find the tape in the library. And there large-as-life was Farrell, the son of a former Shamrock Rovers footballer, dressed in a Glasgow Rangers top wandering onto the stage to be introduced to the assembled media, who hadn't a clue who he was. A theatre press officer said, "Ladies and gentlemen, this is Colin Farrell." He shyly replied with a wave and a "hello there" to us. Within days, Farrell was spotted by American actor and director, Kevin Spacey, who recommended him for a movie. And a star was born.

But spare a thought for Belfast actor, Marc O'Shea, who had played Farrell's part in the initial Irish run of the play. Marc turned down the job in London because he had the chance of going to New York with another production. When I did a story on UTV, having unearthed the rare footage of Farrell at the Donmar, Marc happily agreed to do an interview with me in the Belfast restaurant where he was working as a chef, between acting jobs. I had to applaud Marc's attitude. His day will come.

CHAPTER 14

A Little Acting

The curtain which fell on my academic career at Grosvenor High School in 1969 was also curtains, I reckoned, for my acting ambitions. I didn't think that I would ever get a chance to pursue my dramatic passions after the disappointment of not going to drama school in England, but my big mate, Ron Culbert, who had been in school plays with me, helped to rewrite the script. Ron, a superlative actor, went to Queen's University to study after finishing at Grosvenor. He soon joined the flourishing drama group, Dramsoc, who rehearsed in a little hut in Camden Street, a street made famous in Brian Moore's iconic novel *The Lonely Passion of Judith Hearne*. After several productions, Dramsoc asked their male actors if they knew anyone, even non-students, who would be willing to swell their ranks. So Ron rang me and I was recruited into the cast of a one-act play, *Salome* by Oscar Wilde. It was entered in the Irish universities drama finals at Trinity College in Dublin. Mine wasn't a big role – a guard – yet I had a major impact on the disastrous performance, though it wasn't my fault. One of the other actors was fond of a tipple, and arrived late and a little the worse for wear in Dublin. This meant we were unable to rehearse on the tiny stage for the competition.

As soon as we started, I realised that because I had been directed for a much bigger space, my imposing bulk was blocking most of the action on stage, including a rather sensual dance of the seven veils by the sexy actress who was playing Salome. There was nowhere for me to go and half the audience missed the action. The adjudicator rubbished the production, especially the fact that "much masking was done by the guard at stage right".

Thankfully, however, Dramsoc knew I was innocent and asked me to take part in their main production of the year. After my outstanding brilliance as the third murderer at school in *Macbeth*, I knew I could cope with the role of the second gravedigger in *Hamlet*. At least I was going up numerically in the world of drama, while in the Whitla Hall production, I got to play another role, that of Marcellus. I was something of a scud for Dramsoc. Running onto the stage during one performance, I caught my arm on a piece of scenery which came tumbling down after me.

The previous year, Dramsoc's ranks had included Simon Callow, who was in Belfast for a year's study, and the year before that, Stephen Rea. But *Hamlet* didn't have any such luminaries, though the fight scenes were arranged by Barry Cowan, who was one of the greatest broadcasters in Ireland until his untimely death in 2004. My brief, though seemingly cursed, spell with Dramsoc was still a great experience and a great eye-opener to the wicked ways of the world. My innocent lifestyle with Joan didn't quite match up to the goings-on at after-show parties. I didn't partake in any of it, of course, and my chances to go on acting with Dramsoc were curtailed by my decision to go to work in Portadown. The move put the lights out on my acting career, for a few years anyway, which was a real shame because, in the intervening years, my old schoolmates from Grosvenor set up a former pupils' drama group called Format. They were bursting with ideas, staging great shows like *Sweeney Todd* and *Look Back in Anger*, a production in which I was able to take a small cameo role.

When I moved back to Belfast after my sojourn in Portadown, the stage beckoned again. Format had always wanted to stage Arthur Miller's stirring play *Death of a Salesman*, with me playing the pivotal role of Willy Loman. And so, in 1973, we started rehearsals for what was one of the biggest challenges of my career. Having pulled it off, we followed it up with a much lighter production, Neil Simon's *The Odd Couple*. Surprise, surprise – I was cast in the role of the slobbish Oscar Madison while the other half of the duo was played by Arthur Lowry, a fabulous Felix Ungar. Arthur could have gone on to be a professional actor but the theatre's loss is the oil market's gain. For Arthur is now, I understand, a successful executive in America.

Our odd couple had, several years beforehand, been involved in another school drama, sharing as we did, the ignominy of being sent off during a rare soccer match approved by rugby-mad Grosvenor. I was playing for the prefect's eleven and Arthur was lining out for the Lower Sixth team. Despite the fact that we were buddies, we both lost our heads during the game and the referee, Mr Dalzell, sent us for an early bath. This didn't look good for me, a supposedly responsible prefect, and we both had to explain ourselves to the headmaster. However, we did walk home together after the match.

The theatrical *Odd Couple* was such a success that Format followed it with another of Neil Simon's plays, *Come Blow Your Horn*, in which I was cast as the womanising main character. Playing opposite me was a rather attractive girl called Suzy Smith who had to snog me in what I remember being a rather pleasurable scene. The last I heard of Suzy was that she was the editor of a genteel country magazine in England. Her brother, Paul Smith, made himself billions as the creator of the worldwide hit television series, *Who Wants To Be A Millionaire?*

Sadly for Format, *Come Blow Your Horn* was our last production. Many of our regulars had, by now, followed the exit signs from a troubled Northern Ireland to England while I had changed jobs from the *Belfast Telegraph* to Downtown, where shift work made amateur drama impossible again.

After I joined UTV in 1980 my amateur drama career really took off. It wasn't so much my acting skills that people wanted, it was my sex, or rather my gender. I was a man in a world over-populated by women. My first drama group after Format was a church-based company called St Dorothea's Players from Gilnahirk in east Belfast. My first production with them was *The Flats*, a play about the troubles by John Boyd. It was a dreadfully dull little play but it did give me my first taste of the am-dram festival circuit and the accompanying social whirl. The comparatively few heterosexual blokes were much in demand with the surfeit of females. Naturally, as a married man, I turned my back on any female advances.

In the early 80s, I also took part in summer theatre in Portrush, bringing Joan and Emma along for a holiday. On the festival circuit, I won my first acting award in another troubles play, *Me Oul Segocia* by Stewart Love, and I also suffered one of my biggest embarrassments. My character, Danny, had been blinded and paralysed in a shooting. To act blind I kept my eyes firmly shut behind my dark glasses. I relied on the girl playing my lover to tap me on the shoulder when it came to the interval, as that was the signal to open my eyes and get out of my wheelchair. During one interval at the Group Theatre in Belfast, the curtains got caught and left a huge gap for the audience to see through. Meanwhile, I didn't wait for the tap on the shoulder because I had heard the audience applauding at the end of the first act. I leapt out of my wheelchair and bounded off the stage, much to the amusement of the patrons, who thought they had Lazarus in their midst. This would have been bad enough if the bloody *Belfast Telegraph* hadn't sent reviewer, Jane Bell, along that night. My chagrin was blazed all over the evening paper for everyone to see.

That play also saw me, prior to Danny's shooting, walking off stage for the first, and so far only, time in my career. St Dorothea's, who were a Church of Ireland drama group, had gone to Downpatrick to stage the play about the religious conflict in Belfast in a Catholic church hall. Our visit, unfortunately, coincided with a loyalist band parade through the mainly nationalist part of the town, which was sealed off by hundreds of police and soldiers. The tension in Downpatrick was acute and, even on stage, we could hear police sirens, flute band music and angry shouting. This probably explains why, in the middle of one scene, George Smyth, a gifted actor, and myself lost the run of ourselves. Our characters were supposedly sitting beside a loyalist bonfire as a nationalist mob advanced on them. George's character should have said, "Don't worry, me oul segocia. We'll just sing the 23rd Psalm and the Lord will protect us." But for some reason George blurted out for Danny to sing the 23rd Sash, mixing it up with the name of a loyalist song. I couldn't contain my laughter so I headed off stage and begged Mary McLean, who was playing my mother, to help me before collapsing in a heap. Mary gave me a right dressing down and pushed me back on stage, only now I could hear her roaring with laughter too while George was choking back the chuckles. I bit my lip so hard that I could taste blood. However, George suddenly summoned all his reserve and his character turned nasty, shouting at Danny in a way he had never done before. I knew he was shouting at me, not Danny and the fright helped me, and him, to get back to business and through to the end. Afterwards the parish priest asked us exactly what the 23rd Sash was. He thought it might be some sort of signature tune of a secret Prod society. For years, George Smyth and I have only to look at each other to completely dissolve into fits of uncontrollable laughter.

It was with *The Flats* and St Dorothea's that I experienced for the first time the wonderful world of the Carrickmore drama festival in County Tyrone. We had been used to playing in front of audiences of between seventy and one hundred in festivals like Larne and Portadown. When we went to Carrickmore, or Carmen as the locals call it, I nearly fainted when I saw the number of seats set out in the hall. I asked a committee member how many they were expecting. "About a thousand," she replied. "But if you had been doing a classic Irish play, we would have got a full house." I couldn't wait to get on stage but others among our Protestant church group weren't so enthusiastic. Carrickmore had a reputation at the time as a republican stronghold and nerves were worsened with the murder of a member of the security forces in the area on the day of our arrival. Indeed, an RUC man who was in the cast was stopped by police as we made our way to Carrickmore. The cop who demanded the driver's ID gulped when he saw his police warrant card and learned where we were going. He told our peeler to hide the card in his sock, which he did.

Nevertheless, the welcome in Carrickmore was, quite simply, fantastic. The hospitality wasn't warm, it was red-hot. The very same Prods who had booked rooms in hotels in Omagh because they were too afraid to stay in Carrickmore could not be budged from the pubs until three or four in the morning!

After just a couple of years with St Dorothea's, I spread my acting wings with other drama groups, like the long-established Circle theatre company. At school I had always played the parts of, shall I say, more mature men since my height and girth made it easy to make the transformation. With the Circle, my first role was almost mission impossible because they asked me to play the part of SB O'Donnell in Brian Friel's epic, *Philadelphia, Here I Come*. The character was forty years older than me. I thank my lucky stars for the part because it led, via a circuitous route, to me finding my way into the professional theatre and, more importantly, finding my current partner in life. If I hadn't taken the *Philadelphia* part, I would never have met Joan McCready. She directed the play and would play a major role in my acting career.

One of the set designers for the play was a girl called Siofra O'Reilly from Newry. There wasn't anything between us at that time until fate brought us together again in 1990. Siofra's sister, Emer, was in the cast of *Philadelphia* and I have never felt as sorry for any actress as I did for her. The play was on the syllabus for "A" level students and hundreds of schoolchildren were in the audience at every performance. At two shows in Belfast's Rosemary Street hall the youngsters went crazy, shouting out sexual instructions to Emer which were beyond even my recognition. It was virtually impossible to continue and, at the interval on the second night, we were told that some of the kids were glue-sniffing and throwing up over others in the audience. The schools later assured the Circle that a number of their pupils had been expelled or suspended – news I was able to spread to a wider audience through my contacts with the Sunday newspapers. Many people in the cast – including a prominent judge, John Curran, a leading barrister, Barry Valentine and a top solicitor, Joe Rice – must have thought about packing in the am-dram game altogether. They were encouraged to keep going by Joan McCready and another member of the cast, Noel Linton. He had experienced something similar in another Belfast hall years earlier, at the performance of a Shakespeare play. I recoiled when he named the play as *Much Ado About Nothing*, the venue as the King George the Sixth Centre and the year as 1968. His information left little room for doubt in my mind that my mates and I had been the villains of the piece. I kept my guilty secret to myself.

Joan, wife of the Ulster theatre stalwart Sam McCready, also directed with St Dorothea's, with whom I had maintained my links despite the move to the Circle. Joan asked me to play the lead role in the play, *Harvey*. James Stewart had made the part famous on the silver screen, alongside the imaginary rabbit who was his co-star. As I was heading off to Canada on holiday, I had to turn down the role because I wouldn't have been able to fit in enough rehearsals. Joan asked me to play a small cameo role that didn't require so much work and I agreed. My portrayal of the cranky but worldly-wise taxi driver must have been alright because, a couple of years later, another drama group, St Mark's, asked me to revive it for their festival production of *Harvey* – a production which was to lead to my biggest theatrical break.

Unknown to me, Paddy Ormonde, who was associated with one of Ireland's top am-dram groups, the Clarence Players, saw my performance with St Mark's. As a result he asked me to play the role of Eddie Carbone in Arthur Miller's powerful American tragedy, *A View from the Bridge*. Paddy put together an extremely strong cast and our opening night in the Group Theatre was electric, the best performance of any play in which I had ever acted. In the ensuing festival round, we swept the boards, winning six out of the seven festivals. I won best actor award at the same six events and we picked up loads of other acting and production gongs. Just for the record, the only festival we didn't win was at Newry; instead we came second last. The only comment that adjudicator Jimmy McClatchie made about me was that I should get my hair cut! Lots of people in the Newry audience let us know they were furious with Mr McClatchie. He didn't give us a single award, but after all the success we had, we thought it was a hoot to come away from Newry with nothing. Our smiles broadened

after we won the all-Ireland drama finals in Athlone, the first
northern group to do so in eighteen years. We followed that up by
winning the Ulster final and the European final in Glasgow,
which was the European Capital of Culture in 1990. I took great
delight in telling Mr McClatchie about our achievements the
following year. I bumped into him at the Festival of Light Opera
in Waterford, where I was acting with the First Act Company
from Belfast in the musical *Clown* by the multi-talented Peter
Kennedy. It was my first musical, a new string to my thespian
bow.

Athlone had been a never-to-be-forgotten high, especially the
night of the final adjudication. I was lucky enough to lift the best
actor award and the first thing I did was to phone my parents and
Emma to tell them the news. My father left me speechless by
telling me how proud he was. Just a few weeks later, Emma was in
the audience in the Grand Opera House in Belfast to see me win
the best actor award there too. It was my performance in the
Opera House that got me noticed by the likes of Martin Lynch
and other prominent theatrical folk.

However, I was still an amateur actor without an all-important
Equity card until fate again took a hand in the shape of a phone
call from a former UTV colleague, Peter McAleese. Peter was
working as a producer on a new movie, *Hidden Agenda*, directed
by controversial English movie-maker Ken Loach. Peter said Ken
was looking for a television reporter to play himself in the film,
which dealt with state-sponsored violence in Northern Ireland.
They also wanted my UTV colleague Kate Smith, with whom I
was living by this stage, to be in the film. UTV were initially cool
about the project, fearing the movie would be seen as one-sided,
but Ken Loach flew to Belfast to meet Kate and I, and assured us
that our roles in the film would be completely impartial.
Eventually UTV agreed to let us do the movie but neither Kate

nor I were happy when a Sunday paper ran a story about our involvement in what they dubbed a "pro-IRA film". I was starting to get stick all over the place so I put the word out that I was getting paid £3,000 for a day's work, and even the most extreme Protestant opponents of the film agreed that they would have done it for that kind of money. If only they knew the real fee wasn't even a fraction of that.

The day's filming in England was fascinating. A chauffeur was waiting at Heathrow to whisk me away to a five star hotel in London. Then, the next morning, another driver took me to the set, near the exclusive and refined village of Cobham in Surrey. What the resident millionaires made of dozens of policemen and soldiers swarming all over their village in Land Rovers and tanks is anyone's guess. I arrived on set early in the morning though I didn't get to film my bit – a piece to camera describing a murderous loyalist gun attack on a human rights lawyer from America – until nearly tea-time. However, there were compensations. The catering was excellent and I also discovered I was sharing a trailer with Brad Dourif, an American movie star whom I had admired in a host of movies including *Mississippi Burning* and *One Flew over the Cuckoo's Nest*. Dourif was, initially, quite distant but once he overheard someone saying that I was a real-life reporter in Ireland, he was a lot friendlier. Soon I was answering one hundred and one questions from my new buddy Brad! The female lead wasn't on set that day but the following week, when I accompanied Kate to London to film her scenes, I opened the hotel door to find Frances McDormand, who was later to win an Oscar, recording a scene in the corridor. The cameraman remembered me from seven days earlier and introduced me to her, though he was completely baffled about why I was there.

Kate and I had split up by the time the movie premiered in

London the next year. My new partner, Siofra, and I swanned along to the gala performance with some of her sisters who lived in London. We were almost breathless with anticipation, waiting for my piece-to-camera which I reckoned had lasted nearly thirty seconds. Unfortunately, my big moment was a major let down. Okay, you could hear my voice in the report for nearly half a minute, but Ken Loach had overlaid it with pictures of the other characters watching my broadcast. I was on the big screen for less than three seconds! I had been in *Big Banana Feet* with Billy Connolly for longer, for heaven's sake. There was no way on earth I was going to smooch into the post-premiere party in London after that. Instead we headed straight back to a party thrown by Siofra's sisters. The guests all knew about the premiere and were dying to talk to us about it. Never in the history of mankind has a subject been changed so often by so many people. I consoled myself with the thought that, finally, I was able to get an Equity card on the strength of the movie, opening the door on the world of professional theatre.

CHAPTER 15

Priests, Professionals and Whorehouses

It wasn't the lure of the lucre that made me want to become a professional actor; it was the chance to work centre-stage in theatre here, rather than in the wings. I felt as if I had gone as far as I could in amateur drama. How on earth was I going to better the successes of *A View from the Bridge* anyway? In the meantime, I had embarked on another theatrical venture. Comedian Sammy Mackie asked me to help him set up a new company involving broadcasters from UTV, Downtown Radio and the BBC. His idea was to stage Northern Irish comedies, the likes of which proved so popular for legendary Ulster funny man James Young. It sounded great in theory but I wasn't convinced we would find enough "celebs" who could act. However, Sammy's enthusiasm and energy were boundless as he set about recruiting people who had been actors in another life and before too long we were ready to roll. We settled on the naff name "The Personality Players" and chose a play called *The Quare Gunk*, written by a County Antrim woman, Joyce Minford. The play itself would not have given Harold Pinter any sleepless nights; still, even the title, we were sure, would attract the audience we were targeting – people who didn't normally go to the theatre, or punters who had got out of the habit of watching plays.

John Daly, who was a presenter with Downtown Radio, and myself were cast in the lead roles of Wullie and Shughie, two hapless brothers who needed a woman to look after them after the death of their mother. The plan was to find a wife for big Wullie. He decided to lie in bed under a sheet, pretending to be dead in order to eavesdrop on what his mourners truly thought of him and then pick one of them for a bride. But, of course, every caller hated big Wullie's guts and fancied Shughie instead – well, I did say it wasn't particularly highbrow!

Other cast members included my colleague, and then partner, Kate Smith; plus Trevor Campbell, aka Big T, and his now sadly-departed wife, Lynda Jayne from Downtown. There was also Fiona Poole, sister of the broadcaster, Ronan Kelly. Fiona had had her fair share of fame as the character Annie Largy, who appeared regularly on Downtown. She was a real driving force behind the company while her husband Derek, a builder, constructed the sets. As Sammy had predicted, the formula was a winner. We played to packed houses all over the north, especially in Belfast's Arts Theatre, and as a result we were able to make sizeable contributions to charities like the Northern Ireland Council on Disability and Heartbeat. We discovered we were right: the people who were coming to see the *Gunk* differed from normal theatre-goers – they hadn't been to see a play in ages.

There was one visitor I won't forget – a tramp, or that's how he described himself. I never did find out his name. Anyway, this guy was a real character in Belfast. He slept rough in doorways around the Crescent, close to the Arts Theatre. One night during our run, he set his sights higher than a doorway. A cleaner arrived at the Arts to carry out her normal morning duties and found him fast asleep in the bed I used, on stage. After his rude awakening, he admitted sneaking into the theatre just before the caretaker locked up and hiding behind a door until the last employee had gone. On stage he found my comfortable bed where he spent the night. He also helped himself to eggs and bread, which were used in the play – used, but never eaten, I must add. They would have been mouldy and definitely not fit for human consumption, though they didn't appear to have done our uninvited guest any harm. Talk about a quare gunk. I hit the roof when I heard the news about his exploits. I'm not a particularly precious prima donna but I did demand that the sheets on the bed be changed or I wasn't getting into it. After the clean-up, it occurred to me that this could be a great wee story to plug the play, so I contacted the main newspapers, trying to find different angles for all of them. I got more than I bargained for. I told one paper that we were offering the tramp a VIP ticket for an evening performance; in my innocence, I assumed he didn't read the papers. The following night, he turned up, bold as brass, demanding his ticket. When we found him a seat, the people sitting next to him asked to be moved, but because the play was sold out this was impossible. We were driven to bribery and corruption, and offered our pal a fiver to leave. He replied with a demand for a tenner. We stumped up and he stomped out.

Looking back, I don't know how I managed to meet all my work and drama obligations in 1992, a year which also saw my friend, Stephen McCoubrey, and I produce a ninety-minute video tracing the history of Linfield Football Club. As well as my involvement with The Personality Players, I was acting with the Clarence in a festival production called *The Queen and the Rebels*, while taking my first steps in musical theatre with *Clown*. I also landed my first professional role.

Roy Heayberd was in the forefront of keeping the independent theatre alive in Belfast during the troubles and he offered me a part in a revival of Joe Tomelty's play, *Is The Priest At Home?* He didn't have to travel far to ask me, raising the subject in a queue in the canteen at UTV, where he was working as a director. The play was produced by Theatre Ulster, who operated from the University of Ulster at Coleraine. The production turned out to be a memorable debut for me, as I got to act with the likes of Lalor Roddy, Mark Mulholland, Roma Tomelty, Margaret D'Arcy and JJ Murphy. The discipline and organisation of the professional theatre sharply contrasted with the amateur world. In the am-dram world it was very do-it-yourself, while in the professional theatre there were people to do virtually everything for the actors. *The Priest* played to full houses in the Arts Theatre before heading off around the province. I was like the cat that got the cream as we set off in our minibus to far-flung venues. We also staged the play for a week in Sligo, though not even the priestly connections could attract the crowds there. We couldn't compete with the real thing. The residents of Sligo were far more interested in attending the novena in the church next door to the Hawk's Well Theatre than coming to our production.

Unfortunately that production was to be the last-ever staged by Theatre Ulster and I feared my professional career was over before it had really begun. Then I received a phone call from playwright Martin Lynch. Martin told me he wanted me to take the lead role in a new play by newcomer Owen McCafferty for his Pointfields Theatre Company. McCafferty has gone on to establish himself as one of the hottest playwrights in the British Isles, recently winning three of the top awards in British theatre. Thirteen years ago, however, he was unknown and *Winners, Losers and Non-Runners* was his first stab at writing for the stage. I was curious about why Martin had suggested me for the central role of Gus McMahon. Over coffee, he explained he had seen me in *A View from the Bridge* at the Opera House and paid me the huge compliment of saying he thought I was a better Eddie Carbone than Bernard "Gizza Job" Hill, who had played the part in the West End the following year.

When I read Owen's script, I was blown away; the role of Gus was massive, pivotal to the whole play. It was a good script with Owen's potential shining through. Martin directed the play – his debut in that particular field – and although there were disagreements, I enjoyed the experience and the challenge. Sadly, the play received lukewarm reviews and, after its week-long run at the Old Museum Arts Centre in Belfast, it closed. From my perspective, it was another notch on my professional belt. I later received a lovely letter from Owen thanking me for my efforts and saying that he hoped he could work with me again in the future.

Meanwhile, I was in the musical *Clown,* which was running simultaneously. I played the villainous Philip Coates and sang on stage for the first time. The words and music were written by Lisburn man, Peter Kennedy, who not only directed the show but starred in it and set up the First Act Company to produce it. The standing ovations we received at the Arts Theatre still rank among the most stirring moments in my entire acting career and the boos which greeted my walk-down at the final curtain were simply glorious. The production brought me in contact with Paddy Jenkins, an amateur at the time, who went on to establish himself as one of the best character actors in Ireland. We discovered a shared passion for Van Morrison and have been friends ever since. I particularly like going out with him for a pint because when people would give me stick about "phenomenon", I would pass the buck to Paddy and reveal him as the man behind one of Northern Ireland's most successful TV advertisements, the one for the Fairhill Shopping Centre in Ballymena. Everyone remembers the catchphrase "It's a big shopping centre in Ballymena, heh!"

UTV even asked me to do a story on Paddy after the adverts were decommissioned years later – that's how big they were.

At the start of the summer of 1992, Paddy and I took part in another show with First Act. I played Sheriff Earl Dodds in *The Best Little Whorehouse in Texas*. Unfortunately, my memories of the production aren't happy ones. Just before we were due to open my father died suddenly in the Ulster Hospital at Dundonald. It broke my heart and the last thing I wanted to do was to go on stage to make people laugh. It was my Mum who encouraged me to go on, and not let people down. The opening night was delayed by seventy-two hours to give me time to bury my Dad and after his funeral, I did what my Mum wanted – I went back on stage and finished the run.

More tragedy lay ahead. On June 25, I was having a smoke outside the Arts Theatre when a friend of mine, Anne Maguire, a brilliant journalist with the *Irish Times*, walked past. She said she was going for a drink at a nearby hotel and suggested I join her later. I explained why I wasn't in the mood but she coaxed me to come along. For nearly two hours I talked, and Anne listened, about my Dad. She hugged me at the appropriate moments and promised me that things would get better. Her sensitivity and understanding were uplifting and for the first time in a long time, I actually felt a little bit better. Anne was from Fermanagh and was fascinated to hear about my Dad's love for the neighbouring county of Cavan. She was going home that weekend and offered to dig out books by Cavan writers that would give me a sense of the place. However, on her return journey to Belfast on Monday night, after her weekend in Derrygonnelly, she was killed in a road accident. Her car collided with a lorry near Dungannon. I was devastated when I heard the news. My mother came with me to Anne's funeral which was in Derrygonnelly. The church was overflowing with Anne's family and her many friends. After the service, I drove Mum to Blacklion, which wasn't far away, to leave flowers on the doorstep of my Dad's old church with a little message in his honour.

The musical seemed utterly irrelevant in the wake of all this sorrow, although the cast were magnificent. I will never forget their warmth on the last night of the show when they made a presentation to me. No one said very much about what had happened. No one needed to. After Dad's death, I decided to take a break from the theatre. Then, in early 1993, I was invited to revive my role as the slob Oscar in *The Odd Couple*, a festival production by the Clarence Players. Cast opposite me as Felix was Roger Jennings, a stalwart of the am-dram scene. Roger and I had shared something pretty special in *A View from the Bridge* – a kiss! It took us weeks to get to grips with the idea, and with each other. We kept putting it off until our director Paddy Ormonde could stand it no longer. I knew, there and then, that my first male kiss would be my last. Thankfully Roger and I were able to keep our distance in *The Odd Couple*. The play went down well with audiences and adjudicators, though we didn't win anything, which was a wee bit disappointing and a sad farewell to the festival circuit for me.

In the summer of that year, First Act's Peter Kennedy cast me in another new musical, *The Widow or Bust,* which he had written. Then personal tragedy struck again. Mum, who had battled so valiantly after Dad's death, became seriously ill and was admitted to hospital. Her condition deteriorated rapidly and at the beginning of September, I pulled out of the show. For the next month, my brother Raymond, sister Caroline and I spent most of our time with Mum in the Ulster Hospital. Her pain was dreadful to watch but she bore it with a quiet dignity. Near the end of the month, she surprised us all by asking to see a clergyman. He emerged from a long conversation with her to say she was "ready to go home". Three days later, she said her goodbyes, telling me she loved me and would never forget me, adding that I really was "a wee rascal". I told her I loved her too but didn't really think it time for farewell. However, she slipped into a coma, the end was coming. A doctor advised us to go home for a rest, saying Mum still had a few days. So I drove away to get some sleep but I hadn't driven more than a couple of miles before my pager went off, telling me to return. I was too late. Mum passed away around 11.00am on October 1, 1993, just two days after my forty-second birthday. My siblings and I were shattered. I knew that it would take time to get over my Mum's passing, though I didn't realise just how much of an impact her death would have on me.

CHAPTER 16

Skinny Little

The headline in the *Sunday Life* screamed, NO, I'M NOT DYING! SAYS BIG MAN IVAN, and I nearly did drop dead there and then. It had not occurred to me in February 1995 that I was on the way out. The paper had contacted me after their readers expressed concern at my dramatic weight loss. I had shed at least five stones, leading people to believe I had Aids or cancer. To be fair, pictures of me from that period are scary, I look like a skeleton in a suit but I genuinely didn't think there was anything wrong with me. I told the *Sunday Life* that my new look was the result of a diet I had started after my mother's death.

During her time in the Ulster Hospital my weight ballooned because I was virtually living on hamburgers and chips from McDonalds, across the road. Before she passed away Mum made me promise to lose weight, so I stopped eating junk food and cut down on the booze. As the weeks went by the weight disappeared so quickly that I thought I had discovered a magic formula for fighting the flab. No matter how many pounds I spent on food, holidays and drink, the other pounds still fell off. I had to buy an entire new wardrobe and my weight became a topic of conversation everywhere I went.

UTV were concerned too; they informed me that their surveys of peoples' opinions on UTV's output were as much dominated by my weight as by *Coronation Street*. One woman even thumped me – and I mean thumped – in the middle of the Castlecourt shopping centre and told me I was too skinny. A crowd of baseball-hatted Belfast yobs were particularly callous. As I passed them in Howard Street, they chimed, "Big Ivan has the big C", a reference to cancer. Meanwhile the mirror in my house only reflected what I wanted to see – a new Little. In all honesty, I was kidding myself. Siofra's father, a retired GP, knew something wasn't right. Outwardly I laughed off people's concerns, while inside I was growing more and more concerned the smaller I got. My whole body seemed to be in overdrive. My heart would race and there were times I found it difficult to hold a knife and fork – or a pen – steady in my shaking hands. It was only when I went to see my doctor about another ailment that the corner was turned. The doctor was new to our health centre, replacing my old family GP. By sheer good fortune, I knew him from Grosvenor High School. Bluntly, he told me I looked decidedly unhealthy. I don't know if I would have opened up with anyone else but I described how strange I was feeling inside.

He gave me the once-over and guessed from the look of me that my thyroid gland, which controls the body's metabolic rate, was banjaxed – my word, not his. All the signs pointed to the thyroid being over-active, which explained why I felt my heart accelerating and how the weight was dropping off so fast. He sent me to hospital where a specialist put me on beta blockers and other drugs to balance the thyroid. He told me that the drugs would put the weight back on. I told him I wanted to stay on the thin side. He told me to accept the inevitable. The new smaller-sized wardrobe of suits became the old wardrobe and the old larger-sized wardrobe of suits became the new wardrobe again.

Thank heavens, the mean Cavan streak in me had prevented me from ditching all my old clothes! I continued taking the tablets and having regular check-ups at the Ulster for the next couple of years. They told me if the medication didn't sort things out, I might have to have radio-active iodine treatment, or else the thyroid might have to be removed. Thankfully, the treatment did work and three years later I was given the all-clear with the warning that the problem could resurface in later life.

At one point, I asked the specialist what would have happened if my GP hadn't cottoned on to what was wrong or if I hadn't sought any help. His answer was blunt, "Your body couldn't have coped, and you would have had a heart attack." I also asked him what caused the thyroid to go askew, wondering if my diet had anything to do with it. "Stress," he said. "You must have had a major stressful upset." He worked out a rough timescale in which the stressful incident had occurred, but I rubbished his theory since he said it happened *after* my mother's death – long after. He insisted he was right and when I got home and relayed the conversation to Siofra, she said medical people knew best. Which she would say, I thought. Then, as we discussed the dates the specialist had mentioned, she remembered something I had overlooked – one of the most stressful days of my life, at the end of September 1994. It was the day before the first anniversary of my mother's passing.

My brothers, sister and I kept putting off the sale of our family home in Abbey Gardens because we knew it would be painful and none of us wanted to empty the house of its' past. However, we couldn't put it off forever. After the house was finally sold, we got round to sorting out Mum and Dad's possessions, but that wasn't the hardest part. No, that was saved for when we had arranged for the electricity to be switched off, before the new owners moved in. I was the only one available to let the electricity people in. They told me they would be there first thing in the morning. I got to Abbey Gardens bright and early, thinking I would be away quite quickly. I was wrong. There was nothing in the house, only memories. No chairs, no stools, no telephone. All I could do was sit on the carpetless stairs and wait. And wait. I was afraid to go for a newspaper, in case they called. I didn't have a mobile phone, so I couldn't ring anyone. It was agony, torture. The workmen finally arrived in the afternoon and I left the house for the very last time, thoroughly distraught. When I got home, Siofra said she had never seen me in such a state.

The next time I visited the specialist at the Ulster Hospital, I told him about the saga and asked if that could have been the spark for my thyroid problems. He agreed it was more than likely the trigger. Apparently the simplest of things could upset the thyroid and he cited his own secretary as an example. Her thyroid had gone haywire after a lorry narrowly missed hitting her. After my recovery, I was interviewed by several newspapers about my thyroid problems. In the spring of 2005 a woman in a restaurant came over to thank me for sharing my experiences. Her husband had recognised the symptoms, after reading one of the articles, and sought help. It probably saved his life, she said.

Of course, the sight of me putting weight back on became another talking point but I shrugged off the "fat boy" slagging. I was just relieved to feel normal again and I wanted to do normal things again, like acting. I hadn't thought about acting after my Mum's death but now I was itching to return to the stage. Yet there was no way I was returning to amateur drama, especially not with my old allies in the Clarence Players whose actions would have made Brutus proud. I reckoned I had been a fairly loyal servant to them and to the am-dram movement in general. As well as acting, I had also become the press officer for the Association of Ulster Drama Festivals (AUDF), who organised the annual round of competitions throughout the province. My job was to promote the overall Ulster final in the Grand Opera House and in my first two years I got messages of support from two Northern Irish megastars, Kenneth Branagh and Liam Neeson. They were names that attracted lots of publicity for the finals. We received even more coverage after the Grand Opera House was bombed in 1993 midway through the week of the Ulster final. I covered the attack for UTV at the scene of the blast, and then donned my other hat, as AUDF press officer, giving interviews about the impact on the final, which was hurriedly moved to another venue. I thought I had acquitted myself quite well, so you can imagine my surprise when I drove to Derry for the annual general meeting of the AUDF and a letter of complaint was read out from a drama group, protesting about the lack of publicity in the build-up to the Opera House final. The letter came from the Clarence Players. I resigned on the spot and drove home to Belfast in a state of shock. The only thing that lifted my spirits was a letter soon afterwards from my old friend and director Paddy Ormonde. He wrote that he had known nothing about the Clarence move and was disgusted by it.

I soon bounced back and, along with Sammy Mackie, revived The Personality Players to breathe new life into another old Jimmy Young classic, *All the King's Horses,* by John McDonnell, one of the few Young scripts still in circulation. John Daly and I took the lead roles again in a comedy which looked at the ridiculous divides between north and south and Protestants and Catholics. We were lucky enough to recruit one of Northern Ireland's finest comedy actresses, Olivia Nash, who had appeared with "Our Jimmy" many years before, along with another veteran of laughter, Sidney Dodsworth. We also had an expert set designer on tap, my partner Siofra. The play did great business and we even had to repeat it at the Arts. During the second stint, I made a bad mistake, something I had never done before and will never do again. I had organised a lunchtime meeting with couple of prominent RUC officers for a briefing about a story I was researching. At first I refused their offers of drink because I was due on stage that night, then I relented and agreed to have *one*. But I had one too many and Siofra came home to find me asleep, in the middle of the afternoon. Luckily, there was just time enough for her to pour copious cups of black coffee down my throat. She managed to straighten me out and I got through the show without any real hitches, although I was thoroughly ashamed of myself. Siofra and I went for a meal on our own after the performance, shunning a cast get-together. The DUP politician Nigel Dodds happened to be in the same Chinese restaurant with a group of friends and they applauded as we walked in. Not the normal DUP welcome for a journalist! Then we found out that they had just arrived from seeing the play. I knew Nigel had seen the show during its first run so I asked him which performance he had preferred. He told me that it was much better the second time around.

Around the same time I made my debut in pantomime for Emma's drama group at Knock Methodist Church. She was supposed to be in it too but after I had decided to opt in, she decided to opt out because of other commitments. She was attending auditions for drama schools in England and was offered a place, which she accepted, at the prestigious London Academy of Music and Dramatic Art. She started college in September 1996, just a few days before my own drama career received an unexpected fillip with a phone call from Roma Tomelty who, alongside her husband Colin Carnegie, ran the Centre Stage Company in Belfast. Roma told me they were planning to revive a play by one of the north's most respected writers, Sam Thompson. I immediately thought she was referring to *Over the*

Bridge, a controversial play about sectarianism at Belfast shipyard which had caused a furore in the 60s. But Roma was planning to stage another Thompson play, *The Evangelist* – and she wanted me to play the evangelist, Pastor Earls, a towering tour de force for any actor. I wasn't sure I could do it but Roma had no qualms. Like Martin Lynch she had seen me in *A View from the Bridge* and had adjudicated me in the Ballymoney drama festival, awarding me "best actor". Roma told me that, after I had interviewed her a few months earlier, she knew I was the man to play the part in her new production. I had gone to Garrison in County Fermanagh to do a feature on the Centre Stage summer school and, as I walked towards my car, Roma said to her husband, "That's our Pastor Earls!"

The production was quite something. Since it required a huge ensemble, Roma brought in members of community drama groups from around Belfast to flesh out the cast of professional actors. The character I played was a visiting American evangelist who claimed he could heal the sick. He preached, he bible-thumped and he sang the praises, not only of the Lord but also of himself. The demands of the role were physically and emotionally draining, and to cope with the strains on my voice I sought expert advice from an opera singer. Marjorie Wright, who lived in Warrenpoint, was a seasoned soprano and she showed me how to use my diaphragm to make life easier for my vocal chords.

The rehearsals were exhausting but mighty craic. My oul mucker, Paddy Jenkins was in the cast along with another good mate, Sammy Mackie and the veteran actor Mark Mulholland. Colin Carnegie was the director. We opened at the Arts to encouraging reviews but the real dramas were lurking just around the bend. The first is funny now, though it wasn't then. During one of the long monologues to the pastor's faithful flock, I completely forgot my lines and not because of a memory lapse but because one of the community drama actors, a huge bloke, kept yawning in my face throughout my address, completely throwing me. I grabbed him at the end of the play and told him if he ever did it again, I would throttle him. "You must have known it would distract me," I raged. "Why the fuck did you do it?" Without a second thought, he replied, "Because I was really tired."

Another member of the professional cast made an even bigger impact during one of my sermons. William Walker was one of the most loveable and colourful guys you could ever hope to meet, a great face, a great voice, a great character actor and great company off stage. But he turned up one night with a few sherbets inside him and, during one of the pastor's hellfire and brimstone addresses, I heard a bang from the congregation. As I tried to focus on my lines, I saw a pair of legs being dragged off stage right; Billy had passed out cold. It was near the end of the play and, as he had only one line left, it was agreed that another actor would deliver it for him. No one told Billy. The old trooper in him tried to come on stage at the same time as his replacement to say the same line! I didn't know where to look, though no one in the audience appeared to notice. Sadly, Billy passed away a few months later.

His death tends to overshadow everything else about that production but, leaving that aside, it was an astonishing experience to play the role that legendary actor, Ray McAnally, had created in the first performance of the play at the Grand Opera House in 1963.

Sam Thompson's widow, May, was a great supporter of the Centre Stage production and she gave me a lot of positive feedback about my performance. Her son, Wallace, had a small part in the production. When he told me that his father had been a Linfield supporter, I suddenly remembered seeing him walking down the Lisburn Road after matches and people used to whisper that he was the man who wrote *Over the Bridge*. He was a strange bohemian man, with his wild black hair and checked shirts, and I would never have believed that I would be one day involved in bringing one of his classics back to the Belfast stage.

A month after *The Evangelist* finished, the Grand Opera House rang to offer me a part in their pantomime, *Jack and the Beanstalk*, which featured not just Zippy, George and Bungle from *Rainbow*, but also Su Pollard, of *Hi-De-Hi* fame, Scorpio from *Gladiators*, David Griffin from *Keeping Up Appearances*, and not forgetting the one and only May McFettridge, aka my good mate, John Linehan. I was to marry May seventy-four times during the panto run. and, as ever, our association threw up many laughs on and off stage, including a ridiculous exchange in a pub, which could only have come from the sectarian madland of Belfast. One halfwit, among a crowd of dimwits, who knew I was acting with May in the pantomime, asked me to settle an argument as to whether the lady was Protestant or Catholic. I explained that May didn't actually exist but yer man insisted that she had to be something. I replied she wasn't even a she, that she was a he called John Linehan. This didn't satisfy yer man who then wanted to know what religion May's alter ego was. I told him I didn't know. He would not shut up, so in the end, I said I thought John would be more likely to play the bodhran than the flute. "I told you she was a Taig," shouted yer man to his cronies. "With a name like fucking McFettridge, you couldn't be anything else."

CHAPTER 17

A History of
The History of the Troubles

I could have sworn I was dreaming, standing there in the Tricycle Theatre in London, listening to one of Britain's finest actors, Warren Mitchell, telling me I should give up the day job and go full-time in the theatre business. Mitchell, whose mercurial acting abilities have probably been overlooked because of his Alf Garnett associations, had searched me out in the theatre in June 2003 after the opening night of *The History of the Troubles (accordin' to my Da)*. I hadn't gone to the after-show party with its free bar upstairs in the theatre, because I was busy buying drink downstairs for Emma and her pals, who had come to see the show. They were on a night off from their own show in the Pleasance Theatre, *Have A Nice Life* by Conor Mitchell. Besides, making small-talk on such occasions is not one of my favourite pastimes. I felt a tap on my shoulder as I sat chatting with the actress, Tara Lynne O'Neill, and turned around to face a smiling Warren Mitchell. He was extremely gracious and told me he had enjoyed my performance as Gerry Courtney. He asked what roles I had played before and I told him adding that I was a full-time journalist and part-time actor. He advised me to give up the former and concentrate on the latter. I was completely stunned.

The next thing Enniskillen actor, Adrian Dunbar, star of stage and screen, was shaking my hand in congratulations and I thought to myself, this is some craic. I didn't need drink to get high that night! The Irish comedian Dave Allen was, apparently, another guest on the opening night. I say apparently because I never actually saw him that night, or on other nights when he returned, bringing different friends each time. It's a major regret of mine that I never got to meet him.

It was all very different from my introduction to the play, which was much more low-key. On February 27, 2002 actor Dan Gordon almost collided with me on the stairs of Waterstone's bookshop in Belfast. We got to chatting and he told me that he was working with playwright Martin Lynch and comic duo Alan McKee and Conor Grimes on a new project called *The History of the Troubles (according' to my Da)*. Great title, I thought as Dan explained he was supposed to be directing it but wasn't able to do it now. He added that they were having difficulty casting someone to play the role of the Da, Gerry Courtney. Then it suddenly struck him that I would be perfect for it and said he would have a chat with Martin and the lads. Yeah right, I thought. Four days later, Martin called to ask if I would be interested in playing the part in the new show. I jumped at the chance.

He sent me draft outlines of the play's plot, which centred around Gerry Courtney, his family and madcap circle of friends as they attempted to cope with, and survive, the troubles from their onset in 1969 right up to the present day. It was ironic that I had covered the troubles as a reporter and now I was being asked to feature in a fictional account of what I had seen in all its grim reality. I took three weeks off work to rehearse the play, which had been commissioned by the Cathedral Quarter Arts Festival for just ten nights. On Monday, April 8, 2002 we gathered at the Cooke Centenary Church hall on Park Road to read the script for the first time. The original draft took an incredible two and three quarter hours to read – a tad too long for a modern day piece of theatre. Conor and Alan took sections of the play away to rewrite them after we had discussed and analysed the original text. It took two whole weeks to agree on something resembling the final script, with me acting as an ad hoc consultant on the historical accuracy of the play. After all, I had been there and done that, so to speak. The prospect of getting the play on its feet, with just a week before we were due to open at the Northern Bank building in Waring Street, was frightening. Fortunately, our director, Karl Wallace, was magnificent – a superbly gifted and creative visionary, as well as being a wonderfully calming influence, coaxing and cajoling a little bit here, chiding and scolding a little bit there.

I talked our way into an appearance on my colleague, Gerry Kelly's Friday night show on April 26, where we told a few white lies about our preparedness for the opening night on the following Wednesday. "Have you got an ending for the play yet?" he asked, knowing damned well we didn't because I had told him as much earlier in the canteen. "Oh yes," was our united porky pie; none of us wanted to discourage the public from buying tickets. As it happened, the slot on the *Kelly* show proved to be one of the most significant factors in the early success of the play. Martin, Alan, Conor and I all bounced off each other and big Gerry. It was brilliant television and the next day the box office phone was ringing off the hook. The only downer was that Karl Wallace, who was to join us in the green room after the *Kelly* show, ran into a crowd of yobs on the Ormeau Road and they gave him a kicking. They were exactly the sort of bastards who were in one of the most poignant scenes in the play. Thankfully he wasn't badly hurt and, on the Wednesday, we opened at the Northern Bank with the ending being fine-tuned right up to the last minute. Indeed, just before the audience were allowed in, I was still receiving instructions on a Mick Jagger dance for one of Gerry's drunken scenes.

We honestly didn't know what sort of reception to expect, but we needn't have worried. The one hundred and one people in the tiny venue were loving it: they laughed in all the right places and every time my character went all nostalgic about bars and clubs in west Belfast, many of them joined in, reciting the names of the shebeens like the Cracked Cup and the Happy Flat. When the curtain came down, the audience jumped to their feet and gave us a standing ovation. It took ages to get them out because they all wanted to have a look at the old pictures of Belfast that our designer, David Craig, had used as his backdrop to the action on stage. We knew we had a hit on our hands. Still, the morning after the opening night was a tense time, which is typical with the pressure of putting on new dramatic works. That morning, we gathered at the Northern Bank building for our notes from Karl. Martin wasn't entirely convinced with our script changes. A time out was called by Karl and I wandered around the town for half an hour wondering what would happen next. By the time I returned, peace reigned once more.

Over the next few days, the critics showered praise on the play. The *Belfast Telegraph* called it "a wonderful kaleidoscope of landmarks which have formed battle-scarred Belfast". *The Irish Times* said "this is the genuine article, written with humour and humanity" and *The Irish News* described it as a play of the finest quality and said my performance was "pure theatrical gold dust", which pleased me immensely I must say.

The then Secretary of State, John Reid, came to see the play and afterwards insisted on meeting the cast, telling us he loved it and would tell Tony Blair to go see it if the play ever went to London. He also invited us over to the John Hewitt bar for a drink, much to the consternation of his bodyguards, one of whom had to wait outside in the ministerial car, a couple of hundred yards from where a mini-riot was underway in a nationalist area of the city. Reid's Brazilian-born wife, Carine Adler, gave me a laugh when she said she presumed Conor, Alan and I were all Catholics. I asked her why she thought that and she answered by referring to the nature of the play and its west Belfast setting. I explained that we were, in fact, all actors so our religion, for those of us who had any, didn't come into the equation. It was strange coming from a woman who had directed a soft porn movie in her day – and no, she didn't say she would keep us in mind if she got round to making a sequel!

In retrospect, what was even more surprising than Mrs Reid's comment was the fact that she and her husband were even able to get tickets in the first place. The demand was so great that we were asked to extend the run from the original ten nights to sixteen though it still wasn't nearly enough to keep people happy. I even fell out with friends and relatives who couldn't get a seat and expected me to get them in, which simply proved impossible. One interested observer was Derek Nicholls, the artistic director of the Grand Opera House, who had directed me in panto in 1997. He raved about the play and told Martin that he thought it would be a winner in the Opera House. Sure enough, in June, Martin rang me to say that Derek had made a formal offer to bring the show to the venue.

Personally, after all the exertions and the exhaustions of the *History*, I was keen to take a break but then I got a call from a most unusual source – the BBC! They wanted me to take a role in their popular TV series, *Give My Head Peace*, written by and starring the Hole in the Wall Gang. I couldn't help thinking back to the time of my amateur drama days in the 80s, when the Beeb were filming an excerpt of a play I was in. In the scene they filmed, I was standing with a couple of actors in the background while the dialogue went on at the front. I was stunned when the reporter came over and asked me to turn my back to the camera because of my UTV connections. And now the Beeb wanted me to feature in one of their most successful shows! It was one of three roles I was to play in the series and the parts couldn't have been more ecumenical. In the first episode, I played a loyalist who beat Uncle Andy up. In the second, I was an ex-Provo who gave Da a dig in the bake and in the third, I was a priest. My only regret was that I didn't get the chance to act in a scene with the show's two actresses: Olivia Nash, who had been such a joy to work with in a Personality Players production some years earlier and Alexandra Ford, who had been in an amateur production of *The Odd Couple* with me.

After the first of the three roles I was also recruited by Roma Tomelty's Centre Stage Company for a summer tour in a Sam Cree comedy of all things. Throughout my amateur drama days, I had performed in a couple of Cree plays. I didn't particularly like the humour but the farces did attract the crowds. Roma contacted me to say she was staging a rare professional production of *Married Bliss*, which I had done before with a church group in Portrush. I wasn't exactly euphoric but the chance to act opposite Roma, who would play the dictator-like wife to my hen-pecked husband, certainly appealed. So I agreed and enjoyed the subsequent tour around Northern Ireland – well, most of it at any rate.

The run at the Riverside Theatre in Coleraine almost ran aground. While some actors prefer to sleep around the clock on tour, my journalistic body clock has me up bright and early, and I like to get out and explore my surroundings. On Thursday,

August 15 I decided to drive from Coleraine to Magilligan to try out a new ferry linking County Derry to County Donegal. When I saw the length of the queue of cars waiting to board the ferry, I opted to get on as a foot passenger. The journey was going so smoothly on a blistering hot day that I began ringing around friends and family on the mobile to tell them what they were missing. As I chatted to Siofra, I expressed concerns about the height of the waves, which seemed so out of place on such a glorious day. Just then, a wave almost engulfed the ferry, with water bouncing off cars at the front and soaking people who were outside their vehicles, enjoying the sunshine. I was okay at the back but I noticed parts of the car ramp buckle under the force of the water. The bloke who was in charge of the ferry started swearing at his staff, telling them to get people out of harm's way. The next thing we knew, the lifeboat from Greencastle in Donegal was launched to help us, bringing an older skipper out to the ferry. He needed all his experience and skill to swing the ferry around and reverse it into port, allowing the cars to reverse off from the back ramp. When all foot passengers had disembarked, we were told the blindingly obvious: the boat would not be sailing back to Magilligan where my car was parked. I was stranded. After a couple of hours of panic, the ferry company organised a minibus to take me and the other weary foot passengers, back via Derry to Magilligan. In the meantime, old hack that I am, I had alerted my newsroom and a few others about the drama at sea. The ferry company, naturally enough, were cursing their luck. After hundreds of uneventful crossings, their first problem would be witnessed by a bloody journalist.

On Monday, January 27, 2003 we opened *The History of The Troubles* (*accordin' to my Da*) with a cracking performance at the Opera House in front of over a thousand punters. The play lost nothing of its sparkle in the bigger auditorium. Indeed you couldn't have bought a ticket for love nor money. Going back to the Opera House in the wake of my drama final win there and my run in the panto was a joy. I even got the same tiny dressing room that I had had during *Jack and the Beanstalk*. Conor, Alan and I had agreed that no matter where we played we would always share the same dressing room – for bonding reasons, I hasten to add. So there was nothing else for it – we three big eejits squeezed into that small dressing room for this and all other visits to the theatre. We had the choice of any number of bigger and better spaces but we stuck to the same miniscule dressing room. The staff thought we were mad.

The play went on its travels. After our sell-out fortnight's run at the Opera House, we headed off on tour, starting with a week in the Liberty Hall theatre in Dublin. Audiences there took just a little bit longer to warm to what some of them described as an alien dialect and storyline from a hundred miles up the road. The opening night was a hoot. I was buying a round of drinks at the bar when Martin Lynch wandered over with a vaguely familiar looking man. As I was in the chair, I asked Martin what he and his mate wanted to drink. He introduced his friend as Jim, and only then did I recognise him as Jim bloody Sheridan, the Oscar-winning director! I wanted to shrivel up but Jim stretched out a hand and offered me his congratulations while Martin told me he had been gushing about my performance. This was only getting better.

Also in Dublin, a girl, who had taken part in a question-and-answer session, told us she had a relative who was killed during the troubles. We were relieved to hear she had really enjoyed the play. Later in the theatre bar, my curiosity got the better of me and I had to ask her who her relative had been, just in case I had covered his killing. I knew him rather well. She was a sister of Dominic McGlinchey, the leader of the INLA. I had met his wife, Mary,

who had also been shot dead by rival republicans while the nearest
I had come to McGlinchey was when he walked past me in
handcuffs in the foyer of the Courts of Justice in Belfast and told
me there was anything but justice for him in the building.

It wasn't long after Dublin that I ended up getting even closer
to a whole bunch of terrorists when the lads and I were banged up
in Maghaberry prison for those never-to-be-forgotten
performances I mentioned earlier. Afterwards, people came close
to murder to get their hands on tickets for the magical *History*
tour around the north. In Newry there were complaints in the
local papers about council staff allegedly snapping up tickets
before they went on public sale, which was denied of course. In
Downpatrick, people desperate for tickets took to advertising in
the personal columns of the town's weekly paper. In Warrenpoint,
a man literally chased me as I went to get a meal, begging me to
get him into the show in the Town Hall. He said he was home on
a flying visit from Australia and *had* to see the play. I got him in
to stand at the back.

It was in Cork that we saw empty seats for the first time. If
Dublin audiences had difficulty understanding the dialect, Cork
could have used subtitles. After our first performance in the
Everyman Palace theatre, it was agreed that we should change one
line. In the course of the play Gerry Courtney talked of longing
for "toasted veda", a reference to a malt bread peculiar to the
north. In the bar on opening night, several people approached me
to inquire, "What the fuck's toasted veda?" We changed the line
to "toasted veda bread". Cork enjoyed the play alright but the
response wasn't the usual uproarious laughter we received up
north. We were glad to get back home to places like Enniskillen,
Cookstown, Armagh and Magilligan Jail!

Our most memorable show was in An Cultarlann, the Irish
language and cultural centre on Belfast's Falls Road. Before

curtain-up Conor, Alan and I went into the centre's restaurant for a coffee and found Sinn Féin leader Gerry Adams and his wife Colette having a quiet meal. Gerry told me they were there to see the play. Just after we began on stage, I saw a shadowy figure coming down the auditorium's main steps. My first thought was that he was going to attack Gerry Adams. Instead he walked through the audience onto the stage, where he dodged between me and Conor, striding into the curtained area at the back. We tried to keep the play moving but had to stop after there was an almighty bang from behind us. We ran off the stage to discover that the intruder had knocked over a massive speaker and was now trying to remove his clothes. A number of officials frog-marched him away and we kick-started the play again. Later, we were told our space invader was an epileptic. He had felt a fit coming on and needed to get out of the theatre immediately. As Alan McKee said to the audience in a rapid-fire ad-lib, we were used to people walking *out*, not walking *on*.

In June, it might have been better if some people – the critics – had never walked *into* the show at the Tricycle in London. While most of the paying public loved the show, many of the newspaper reviewers hated it. Perhaps we should have expected the Tory *Daily Telegraph* to lead the onslaught. Charles Spencer said that he had rarely left a show feeling such contempt for those involved. He ended his review by calling us fellow travellers with terrorists. To even hint that the play was a propaganda piece wasn't just offensive – it was total nonsense. This was a play which had been enjoyed by people in *every* part of the province. The reason why it was so successful at home was that it managed to plough a straight furrow, condemning *all* violence from *every* source. It provoked only *laughter* from audiences of all religions, not at the plight of the victims, but at the hilarious and ridiculous happenings on the periphery of the troubles, showing how we coped with lunacy. I think another reason for the play's success was down to its' humanity. Gerry Courtney was Everyman, a man of strength and courage whose family came first. A west Belfast Catholic, yes; a nationalist, yes; but his yearning for peace and his concern for his family's safety could equally have been the values of an east Belfast Protestant, a unionist. That's not to say Gerry was Pa Walton. His views about Maggie Thatcher verged on murderous intent; they were even quoted in a major *Sunday Times* colour magazine special edition about the former Prime Minister. However, nationalists didn't have a monopoly on dislike for Maggie in Northern Ireland as Prods hated her too. In general, Gerry stood for everything that was, and is, good about Northern Ireland. Mr Spencer seemed shocked by the concept of using humour in a play about the troubles. He just didn't get it. Laughter was one of the main things that got us through the nightmare, that and our ability to take the piss out of ourselves, even at the worst of the bad times.

The *Evening Standard* also loathed the play, with Nicholas de Jongh writing that "the lumbering triviality of Lynch's superficial trawl through Northern Ireland's awful recent history left me unaffected and unamused". He did, however, have nice things to say about me: I had acted with a sensitivity and sensibility that "this raucous revue" scarcely deserved. A pity that he spelt my name wrong but hey ho. The reviewer from *Time Out* magazine, Dominic Maxwell, called me *Ivan Lytle* when he wrote about my "fine performance as Gerry, giving him a compelling flawed dignity".

Despite the damning reviews, the Tricycle's highly-regarded boss, Nick Kent, wanted us to extend the one-month run. None of us were overly keen, especially Conor whose wife Joanne was expecting a baby that summer. We had also been offered the chance to perform at the Edinburgh Festival, but again we had to turn it down. I loved the London theatrical experience and an added bonus was Emma also acting in town, which was a fortuitous coincidence. I had taken her regularly to London as a wee girl to cram in as many shows as possible and we were always avid theatre-goers during her time at college there. Now here we were, both of us involved in theatrical productions in the same place at the same time. If I wasn't catching up with Emma during the day, I was working for UTV as their de facto London correspondent. I had, for the first time, encountered the double agent Kevin Fulton while I was covering a political story for UTV at the House of Commons. He kept me busy, providing me with a blow-by-blow account of his battle to stop the authorities throwing him out of his safe house.

I wasn't sorry to get home at the end of the Tricycle ride. I enjoyed doing the play but London exhausts me and, after a while, the sheer size and pace of the place starts to irritate me. This was one of the reasons I never sought a job with ITN at any stage of my career. As soon as I reported back to UTV in 2003 I was sent to another place I have since grown to detest: Drumcree, in Portadown, to cover the by now annual row over the walk by Orangemen down the Garvaghy Road. God, how I longed then for London!

There was to be no stopping the *History of the Troubles*. It has been revived again and again, setting a box-office record at the Grand Opera House, where it played four sell-out runs. What was supposed to be a ten-night run in front of a thousand people at the old Northern Bank building has turned into an almost unparalleled success story. We have played to nearly one hundred and fifty thousand people across the British Isles, in one hundred and eighty-one performances, from the biggest venues like the Opera House to the smallest, such as loyalist clubs in east Belfast and republican venues in west Belfast. In those clubs we performed on tiny stages, completely surrounded by the audience.

The play has won several awards, but more importantly it has brought thousands of people to the theatre. It's a rare day that goes by without someone mentioning the play to me or someone wanting to know where Conor's character, Fireball, is. People are always asking me if the play is coming back. They live in hope. So do I.

CHAPTER 18

Phenomenon

The impact has been nothing short of phenomenal. I never imagined that giving my approval for UTV to show the clip of me trying to say that bloody word, phenomenal, would change my life, but it has. If you don't know what I am talking about, the out-take has been shown on countless blooper shows at home and in Britain. It is no exaggeration to say that, for every day of my life, since it was first aired, and even in places like Barbados and New York, someone has either asked me to say *that* word or ribbed me about my inability to master it. Yet when I was first approached by UTV's senior director, Robert Lamrock, for permission to use the blooper in a 1997 programme called *Get it Right Next Time* I didn't have a baldy notion what he was talking about. He had been tipped off by our library staff that the foul-up might be worth using in the show, but I couldn't remember it. However when it was played to me, I had to agree it was really funny.

It was on August 2, 1995 when the phenomenon started. I had gone to Linenhall Street in the centre of Belfast to record an interview with Ulster Unionist politician, Jim Rodgers, who had issued a statement urging traffic wardens in Belfast to lighten up a little. He claimed they were over-zealous and were frightening tourists away from Belfast, at a time when the ceasefires were beginning to give foreigners more confidence to visit. I thought the story was just the ticket to get my puns out and, after the interview, I decided to film a couple of reversals, which is when the cameraman records the reporter asking his questions so they can then be edited into the chat. One of my questions kicked off with "But surely traffic wardens aren't just a Belfast phenomenon?" A group of workmen on a nearby building site were taking great delight in shouting out my name, trying to put me off, and no matter how hard I tried, I simply couldn't say "phenomenon". I kept saying "phenomenum" and creasing myself up with laughter. Cameraman Albert Kirk suggested alternative words like "problem", but that only sent me into more convulsions and after trying ten or twelve times in three or four minutes I gave up. My question became "But surely traffic wardens aren't peculiar to Belfast?" Problem solved; or so I thought.

As it happened, *Get it Right Next Time* was broadcast in December 1997, during my run in the Grand Opera House pantomime, *Jack and the Beanstalk*. Playing opposite me was Belfast's favourite housewife May McFettridge, my great mate John, one of the quickest and most wicked ad-libbers in the business. I knew that after the bloopers programme he would try to ambush me on stage, so I spent an hour perfecting the way to say "phenomenon". I contacted the director Derek Nicholls and asked to make a slight change to my opening line on stage. The line was a nod to my other life as a news reporter and I changed it to say, "Good evening everyone. Tonight, as usual, I bring you the news but tonight's news is quite phenomenal." Half of the audience must have been watching the night before because I got lots of laughs and applause, and the look on May/John's face was a picture. He told me afterwards that he and another comedian in the show, John Evans, had worked out a routine to poke fun at me and my phenomenal problem. I upstaged the buggers!

It wasn't too long before everyone else in Belfast wanted to have their say; whether I was walking down the street or sitting in a café, someone would have a go at me. Years later, it's like water off a duck's back, I have learnt to smile through gritted teeth and play along with it all. Just so long as people are polite and upfront. Some folk can be downright ignorant so I tend to blank them completely. Invariably, it's the supposedly better educated and affluent who are the rudest. In a shopping centre in Bangor, a group of five or six of the most obnoxious ladies-who-lunch types caught me on a bad day. They thought it hilarious to shout out their barbs behind my back but my response was more than a match for the colour of their blue rinses.

There was the time in the King's Square shopping centre in east Belfast when this bloke, sporting a Cherryvalley accent, said to his female companion, "Look, it's the man from UTV who can't say synonymous." He proceeded to break it down into smaller sections, virtually spitting in my face, "SEE-NON-EE-MUS", adding with a patronising giggle, "It's so simple." "Yeah, I'll remember that," I said. "Pity the word I had difficulty with was 'phenomenon'. That's the word with which I am sy-non-y-mous."

One of the more inconsiderate encounters was in the canteen of the Daisy Hill hospital in Newry. I was having a cup of tea with Siofra just after her Dad had been admitted. It was obvious from her red and tired eyes that she was extremely upset. Despite that, a hospital employee, who had been sitting with his colleagues, came over to our table and thrust a piece of paper into my hand, waiting for me to read it. I told him where to go when I realised the note said, "It's phe-nom-e-non".

Most people are fine: the majority of folk really believe they are the first to say "phenomenon" to me but sure, it's just a bit of fun. One of the most hilarious incidents came as I hurried down Chichester Street in Belfast after covering a republican rally at the City Hall. You know when someone is going to say something, and I had no doubt that the approaching chancer was psyching himself up. However, he lost his courage and walked past. From a safe distance, he turned and shouted, "You're a big eejit, big man. Sure the word is PHERMOMETER!" I still go into kinks about yer man even now, and about the spides in the Castlecourt shopping centre who shouted, "Yee-ha, Ivan – it's PSYCHOLOGICAL!"

Not so long ago, after I had finished interviewing Colonel Tim Collins – of the Iraqi eve-of-battle speech fame – in the Europa Hotel, a stills photographer Mark McCormick, who was waiting to snap him, overheard a conversation between two women sitting nearby. One of them said, "That's your man isn't it? Him that can't say that word." Her friend asked her what word she meant, and she replied, "Fermanagh"!

Then, one Saturday morning, I walked into UTV just as the strangest looking people were gathering for an Elvis Presley lookalike competition on the *Kelly* show. This tiny man, with a massive belly dangerously stretching his Elvis jumpsuit, guldered from beneath his ill-fitting wig and ridiculous sunglasses, "Hey, big fella, what about the phenomenon then, eh? You big doughbeg ye." I took one look at him and said, "Excuse me. *You're* taking the piss out of *me*?" Crestfallen, the man who would be King abdicated there and then.

Even the paramilitaries have had a pop. In a darkened room in Rathcoole, I found myself facing a group of five UDA men, all wearing balaclavas and fully armed. A gruff voice barked at me, "You have been asked here today, Mr Little, to hear a statement from the leadership of the UDA. You may take photographs but you may not record sound. You will be given a copy of the statement afterwards. You will not be allowed to ask any questions and you will be expected to leave promptly after the reading of the statement." Which is exactly what I stood up to do at the end of the publicity stunt. As I put my hand on the doorknob, the same voice boomed from behind his balaclava, "Mr Little?" I turned around quickly and he asked, "Can you say 'phenomenon' yet?" This provoked feverish guffaws from them and a perfect pronunciation of the word from me. It was probably the sight of all that weaponry which perfected my delivery.

My new-found fame also brought me in contact with the Provisional IRA leadership. During a flying visit to Bundoran in County Donegal, I had lined up three interviews with people protesting against plans for a march by republicans. It was a rush job – I had to get back to Belfast to edit – so I asked all three interviewees to be at the same place at the same time. As I jumped back into my car, a van blocked me in. The driver told me the republican leadership in the town wanted to give me the IRA perspective, and he drove me to a house where a man outlined why the Provos wanted to march. As I left, I said I was amazed at the Provos' intelligence because I had only been in Bundoran for a short time. One of them replied, "No, it was my daughter. She passed you on her school bus as you were doing your interviews and she told me that the man who couldn't say 'phenomenon' was in town. I put two and two together as to why you were here, and that's why we sent for you."

The out-take has also opened doors and got me interviews where other journalists have failed. Most notably, during a loyalist feud on the Shankill, when the owners of a shot-up house invited me into their home, ignoring all other reporters outside. The family said they would do an interview with me if I let them video me saying "phenomenon".

Days later, on the Springfield Road, I was trying to take cover during a riot by nationalists. A man recording the events for the local community group turned his camera away from the action and asked me to say "phenomenon" so he could include it in a piece for a forthcoming festival. I replied with "This is Ivan Little for *UTV Live* at the scene of a phenomenal riot on the Springfield Road." It cheered him up no end.

What cheered me up was when Emma and I were having a drink with John Linehan in the Europa hotel and actor James Nesbitt walked in. John asked Emma if she would like to be introduced to Nesbitt and off they went. In the middle of the conversation, I heard Jimmy say, "Ivan Little's daughter? Mr Phenomenon, where is he? I want to meet him." And for the next two or three hours Jimmy and I chatted like old friends about the relative merits of Linfield and Coleraine football clubs.

During another late-night drinking session in a hotel in Portstewart, an Australian man came over to me and asked if I was the bloke who couldn't say "phenomenon". I wondered how on earth he knew about my little problem. "It's shown on our bloopers shows back home," he replied, "and my relatives, who live here, confirmed my suspicions you were the guy and dared me to speak to you."

But "phenomenon" has also led to confusion. Once, as I sat in my car waiting to make a right turn, the driver in the car on my left waved frantically at me to roll down my window. Thinking I knew what he wanted, I shouted over to him, "The word's phenomenon." He looked baffled and said, "What? Sorry, I was going to ask you to direct me to Bedford Street."

A repeat performance came in Manchester after a visit to the shops in the city centre. I went in to buy a paper and the man behind the counter said, "Excuse me, but how do I know your face? Where have I seen you before?" Stupidly, I told him I worked in television and mentioned the bloopers programmes, to which he replied, "No I have never seen you on the television." Then he suddenly remembered, saying, "Oh, I've got you now. Weren't you shopping in Marks and Sparks a few hours ago? You were. I remember you because you are so tall." Talk about being cut down to size!

The "phenomenon" clip isn't even my favourite of all the out-takes which have featured on local and national television. I prefer the one where I jumped out of my skin after a wee dog snapped at me in Lisburn. I was doing a follow-up piece on the hungry hound at his new home on the back of my earlier report on how he had been dumped in a bin, and his way of thanking me was to sink his teeth into me.

Another one I liked was of me effing and blinding outside the Rostrevor home of Mary McAleese after she had been confirmed as the new President of Ireland. The normally quiet village was deafening that day, with cars and lorries pumping their horns, and I replied with a four-letter rant, calling Rostrevor the horniest place in Ireland. Several years later, I had the privilege of introducing Mrs McAleese at the *Andersonstown News* group's Aisling Awards and I couldn't let the occasion go by without formally apologising to her from the stage for turning the air blue outside her former home.

Another clip, which is repeated endlessly on national television, is when I had a problem with a technician before a Simply Red concert in Belfast. Unfortunately for me, he was doing his sound-checks at the same time as I was trying to record a piece-to-camera. Every time I opened my mouth, he shouted, "One two, one two" or "Sarah, Sarah, Sarah". Wearily, I groaned, "Fuck Sarah", and another naughty blunder was born.

Another out-take, which people seem to enjoy, is the one where I scared the living daylights out of a group of pigs! My report concerned how a Tyrone farmer had come up with the novel idea of holding pig races for fairs and shows with a specially constructed track and little jumps. I thought it would be a good idea to stand in the middle of the track and do a piece-to-camera as the pigs raced around it. However, as the little porkers approached yours truly, they took one look at me and, instead of running on by, turned on their trotters and raced back from whence they came. It was hilarious.

Without doubt, my best TV out-take hasn't even been seen on the small screen yet. I was doing a piece-to-camera in a Tyrone town when the local "character" came along. He was pretending to be a cowboy and ordered me to get out of town. After firing a pretend gun at me he told me I didn't walk right. So I strolled up and down the street with the camera still running while he tried to coach me on how to walk like John Wayne. It is absolutely hysterical but UTV can't broadcast the clip without the permission of the cowboy and, as yet, that has not been forthcoming.

I must say, in my own defence, most of the out-takes with which I am now associated weren't actually bloopers or mistakes. Only the "phenomenon" episode was truly a cock-up. All the other out-takes were just funny or peculiar happenings which, funnily and peculiarly enough, happened to me when there was a camera around.

However, my favourite mistake of all time went out on the radio. Never can a mix-up of words have been more appropriate. I was reading the news at Downtown one afternoon and came to a story I had written myself about a fire at a butcher's shop on Belfast's Oldpark Road. The police told me they thought the fire had been started deliberately. As I read out the story, I must have had the word "maliciously" in my head and I came out with the immortal line, "Police believe the fire in the butcher's shop was started *deliciously*."

It was at Downtown that I managed to muck up the name of the place where the *Titanic* was built. No, not Warland and Holffs! I was warning drivers to avoid the Sydenham by-pass because of tailbacks and I said that Bangor-bound traffic was stretched all the way from the Tillysburn roundabout to the entrance of the *shityard*!"

CHAPTER 19

A Little Confused

"One Ivan Little, there's only one Ivan Little," sang the Northern Ireland fans as I stepped up to take – and miss – my charity penalty kick before a Windsor Park soccer international. They were wrong. There would appear to be dozens of us, in dozens of variations. When you are big, bearded and bulky, it's quite amazing how many people mistake you for somebody else.

Take the day in January 1996 when I was reporting on a killing on the Falls Road in Belfast. The murder victim was Gino Gallagher, a leading figure in the INLA, and the full press corps were out to cover the story. As we stood together outside the dole office where Gallagher was murdered, a little lad of about eight or nine walked up to me with a piece of paper and pen in his hand. "Can I have your autograph please?" he asked politely. "Certainly," I replied, grinning at my journalistic colleagues. "Who will I sign it to?" I asked the wee lad. "Michael," he answered. With a flourish for the rest of the hacks, I wrote, "To Michael, with regards and best wishes for the future, Ivan Little, Ulster Television, Belfast." At the time, I was on the skinny side, thanks to my thyroid problems, and I was wearing my silver-rimmed glasses. Bewildered I watched as the youngster read my autograph and then ripped it up, to the amusement of the press pack. "But here, son, you asked me for the autograph, why did you tear it up?" I asked. He didn't even try to disguise his disgust as he grunted, "I thought you were Gerry Adams."

It's not an uncommon mistake. Several newspapers even reported on the schoolchildren, touring Stormont with former Agriculture Minister Brid Rodgers, who rushed towards me with autograph books, as I stood in the middle of the press pack. "Who's that?" screeched their classmates, standing on the steps of Parliament Buildings. "Gerry Adams," came the reply, before a highly amused Brid put them right.

It wasn't the first or the last time Brid and I had a laugh together. For several years at Drumcree, during the height of the Garvaghy Road controversy, I had to interview her live on television. The best place to conduct interviews at Drumcree was at the top of a cherry-picker hoist, which could soar sixty feet above the ground. The vantage point gave the cameraman the perfect shot of the interview, framed against the church with the Orangemen in the background. The only drawback was my irrational fear of heights. So Brid would hold my hand as our cameraman, Donovan Ross, who also operated the hoist, sent the two of us climbing higher and higher. The interviews were bizarre. The viewers could see and hear me throwing tough and pointed questions at Brid about the SDLP stance on Drumcree while keeping a firm grip on her hand. She never held back on her forthright answers but, to be honest, I didn't give a hoot about what she was saying. All I cared about was that she didn't let go of me and getting back down to earth.

On the lookalike front, one of the funniest mix-ups came in Dublin when dozens of other journalists and myself assembled for a press conference by American country star, Garth Brooks. I have to admit that Chris Roche, the PR who organised the event, could be my twin. As time wore on, the singer's manager pulled me aside, furiously demanding to know why the press conference hadn't started. I shrugged that I had no idea, it was nothing to do with me. This did little to calm him and he gave me a right rollicking, saying it was my job to know. All of a sudden, the penny dropped. "Who do you think I am?" I asked the boss man. He replied, "You're Chris Roche." "Nope, I'm a journalist from Belfast," I responded, causing him to splutter out an embarrassed apology.

A few hours later, it was my turn to nibble humble pie in the hotel where I was staying. After the confrontation with Brooks' manager, I was called away from the press conference by my bosses and told to interview the Taoiseach, Albert Reynolds, who was attending the gig. UTV and ITN wanted his reaction to a three day ceasefire that the Provisional IRA had just called. Eventually my cameraman and I tracked Albert down and he was only too happy to share his views. By the time we got the interview played down the line to Belfast and London, we had missed the show and so I returned to the Berkeley Court Hotel. As I went up to my room, a balding Yank in the lift asked me if I had enjoyed the concert. I explained I hadn't been able to go because of the ceasefire and asked him if he had been there. "Well yeah," he replied, "I was playing in it. Don't you remember? You interviewed me before I went on stage." It was only Garth Brooks himself! I didn't recognise him because he wasn't wearing his Stetson. Mortified, I tried to apologise but he was too busy laughing to hear me. When I got to my floor, he said, "By the way, congratulations on the ceasefire." As if it had anything to do with me!

Chris Roche has since passed away but we loved the confusion we caused at concerts. We would swap stories of who thought which of us was which. I stopped counting the number of requests

I got for free tickets from journalists in the south.

Not all of the mistaken identity incidents have been funny, however, especially not the confrontation which happened in an east Belfast bar when I was enjoying a drink with a group of friends. Out of the blue, a scary looking thug pushed his way through and screamed in my face, "Fuck off, ya bastard. You're not wanted in here." My mates tried to reason with the moron, telling him I was only in for a quiet jar and didn't want any trouble. We all assumed he knew me from the box until he called me a "beardy Fenian bastard from Coleraine". He had me confused with someone else. "Who do you think he is?" asked one of the lads. "I know exactly who he is, he's that ugly big fucker Magee," he said. I didn't know whether to laugh or cry; he thought I was a bloke who been goalkeeper for Coleraine FC years ago. One of the lads told yer man my real identity, which only set him off on another one. "Aye right, I know you now," he said, "and sure you're a bastard too."

While we're on the subject of silly buggers: what about the daft policeman who was waiting for me to return to my car after I had foolishly parked it in a control zone? This was the late 80s and as we all know, control zones were areas where motorists couldn't leave their vehicles, in a bid to thwart the bombers. "Oh, it's you!" the cop exclaimed, loudly enough for the world and his wife to hear him. "You would think that with all the terrorist attacks you have covered on UTV that you would know where you can and cannot park your car." On and on he went, loving every second of his lecture. Blushing, I admitted I had screwed up badly. He said he would have to give me a ticket for the offence and asked for my driving licence. Cursing the arrogant bollox under my breath, I agreed he had no alternative and accepted my punishment like a man. When I got home and read the ticket I saw that, even with my driving licence in his hand, the peeler still managed to book me in the name of Robert Ivan *Martin*, mixing me up with the Downtown Radio presenter. I immediately rang the RUC Press Office to inform them of their colleague's cock-up, only to be told to send the ticket to them and forget all about it. They said they would pass it on to PC Plod's commander for him to deal with it. I wish I could have seen the sickly smile wiped off that smarmy copper's face.

The smile on *my* face, on holiday in Portugal in the 80s, was as broad as the Algarve coastline. I was dining in a restaurant with Emma when a gorgeous-looking American woman, dripping in wealth and glamour, came over to inquire if, as she was convinced, I was Kenny Rogers, the American country singer. I fought the temptation to burst into *The Gambler* and told her the truth. However, she didn't believe me. She thought I had to be, at least, Kenny's kid brother.

It might not be too surprising that people get me muddled up with Ivan Martin, Gerry Adams and even Kenny Rogers, but Adrian Logan? We're about as alike as May McFettridge and Pamela Anderson. Still, there's one wee girl in a Portadown housing estate who couldn't tell us apart. I had just left a house after filming an interview in the Killicomaine estate when the young lassie, who must have been about eleven or twelve years of age, ran up to my car. "You're Adrian Logan, aren't you?" she smiled. "No, actually I'm not," I countered. "Yes you are, you're Adrian Logan," she persisted. "You do that oul Gaelic football on the television." I stood my ground. "Honestly, I'm not Adrian Logan, but I do work in the same office as him." "So what are you called?" she asked. I told her. "Rubbish," she said. "Ivan Little's the one that can't say 'phenomenon'." I told her I *was* the one who couldn't say 'phenomenon'. "But you've just said it," she hit back. "I know," I wearily agreed, "I've learnt how to say it now." She wasn't convinced and turned away, before asking for my autograph. "But you don't know who I am," I laughed. However, I signed a page from my notebook and passed it through the window. "Ach, no," she snapped. "Sign it Adrian Logan, not Ivan Little." I dutifully scrapped the first one and signed another one, "With love from Logie." Anything for peace.

I remember another day when I was enjoying the sun in Warrenpoint and another girl asked for my autograph for her mother, who was sitting down the street. I waved at Mum and signed her book. No problem. Within minutes, the girl was back with a face on her. "My Mummy's all disappointed," she explained. "She thought you were Bob Monkhouse."

Now Bob and I weren't exactly separated at birth or anything, but what could I do? I sent my apologies down to the mother for not being the popular British comedian and quiz-show host.

Another incident from the file marked "stranger-than-fiction" was the conversation I had in the lower Shankill area in Belfast during a feud between the UDA and the UVF. I was walking towards my car when I heard my cameraman telling a couple of young lads that my name was Ivan Little and that I was a reporter with UTV. "So who did they think I was?" I asked him. "Tony Blair," he replied. I told him to wise up but he insisted it was true. I had to have a word with the kids myself, and yes, they did believe I was Tony Blair; but they scampered before I could discover if they knew who Tony Blair was or what he did for a living.

In my slimmer days, I once heard a couple of girls outside Boots in Belfast, speculate on whether or not I was Barry Gibb from the Bee Gees! Then, *inside* Boots, at the photographic counter, two assistants were arguing about my colleague, Gloria Hunniford. The girls were sure that Gloria was having an affair with a colleague in UTV – which was total crap – but they just couldn't agree on her paramour's identity. They discussed a variety of men in the building until one of them said, "No, a friend of mine told me that it's definitely Ivan Little." And there I was, standing right in front of them, and they hadn't a clue why I was laughing my head off.

Neither did the Elvis impersonator, Frank Chisum, catch on to his slip-up one New Year's Eve in a hotel in the wonderful village of Glencolmcille, County Donegal. My sister Caroline and her husband Robin had a cottage in the valley, but they stayed in the hotel that night so that they could enjoy the party and still check on their kids. In the foyer, Caroline got chatting to Frank, who was telling her how he had big-name fans all over Ireland and the UK. I had only been in the company a few seconds when he said to Caroline, "Here, wait till I tell you who was in the audience here tonight. You know yer man who does the news on UTV, Ivan Little? He was here, so he was." He was looking straight at me as he said this. Obviously, someone had told him I was there but he didn't know me from Adam and I didn't have the heart to put him right.

It was in another part of Donegal, close to the village of Clonmany, that I was privileged to hear a textbook example of Irish logic. As I joined a queue for the ATM, a guy in front asked me, "Aren't you that fella from UTV, Ivan Little?" I told him he was right and he said, "You know, you don't look like yourself at all." Quick as a flash, his mate, who had been standing with him, piped up, "Well, how the fuck do you know it's him then?" Silence was the only reply.

I was similarly struck dumb by an incident just before the final of the Heineken Rugby Cup in Dublin in 1999 when Ulster beat the French side, Colomiers, at Lansdowne Road. I had been brought to the match as a guest of a bank and, after swallowing the finest food and wine at a pre-match reception, we all set off for the game. I got separated from the rest of the journos and ran into a group of Ulster fans from Portstewart who seemed shocked to see me. One of them gasped, "Jesus, you're the *real* Ivan Little", which baffled me no end. They then explained that their mate was my double and also a namesake, Ivan McGrotty. I laughed it off but they pointed to my doppelganger, who had just caught up with us. I turned around and nearly fell over. It was like looking in a mirror – same hair, same beard, same nose, same bloody everything. My spitting image told me people always mixed him up. Only minutes beforehand, in a Ballsbridge pub, a crowd of Ulster fans were shouting my name at him.

A few months later, this Ivan bumped into that Ivan again, in a bar near Portstewart. This time I was with Siofra, who had thought I was just exaggerating the Dublin story. When she met the other Ivan she became a believer. At the end of the night, she was up on the dance floor jiving with Ivan 2 and, as I caught sight of the two of them, it was like an out-of-body experience: I was watching myself dancing with my lady!

As I've already said, I was frequently confused, in my slimmer days, with Gerry Adams. Not so long ago, I almost got the chance to play Gerry Adams on the silver screen. A theatrical agent rang me to say that a film company wanted to audition me to portray the Sinn Féin leader in a drama about the Omagh massacre. I thought they had to be kidding. Okay, in the days of yore, when I was a lot thinner, I might have been able to carry it off, but I knew the bigger Little hadn't the slenderest of chances of getting the job. However, a casting agent travelled up from Dublin to audition and videotape me reading several lines of script from the West Belfast MP.

That night, I met a friend for a drink and told him what I had been doing that day. "Gerry Adams?" he sqawked "You playing Gerry Adams? You've no chance, big man. The size of you – you look like you've eaten him!"

CHAPTER 20

A Little Blue

I thought I had died and gone to heaven: Blue Heaven. It was 1982 and I was travelling with the Linfield team on their bus from the Oval in Belfast to the lounge at Windsor Park for a celebratory meal, with the Irish Cup perched on my knee. Twenty years earlier, I'd had my first fleeting but glittering glimpse of the seven trophies won by Linfield in a clean sweep of the Irish League competitions. My brother Norman had for some reason been invited to the trophy room and I had slipped in too. Now, two decades on, I was admiring the silverware in my own right – a perk of my part-time "job" as joint editor of the Blues' match day programme, *Look at Linfield*. I had accepted an invite in 1978 from former Portadown journalistic colleague, Billy Kennedy, to help produce the programme after the resignation of the late lamented BBC journalist Rupert Miller. The programme won a series of awards in various British competitions and, in 1980, Billy and I were also honoured with a special merit award for our work on the publication, as well as the Northern Ireland international team's programme, by the Professional Footballers' Association.

Editing the programmes meant that I had a virtual "access all areas" pass at Windsor Park. I could wander in and out of the

Linfield dressing room, and I developed a great rapport with colourful characters like Peter Rafferty, George Dunlop, Lindsay McKeown and my oul mate Billy Murray. I was privy to a host of stories from that lot, though only the positive ones were used in the programme, of course.

As well as hanging out in the players' lounge after matches, I had an open invitation for a pint into the normally closed-shop Linfield boardroom too. It was hardly a secret that Linfield operated a "Protestants only" policy for their playing staff in those days. It was an unwritten rule but a rule nonetheless, one that the footballing authorities, supporters and the media turned a blind eye to – even nationalist politicians kept their own counsel for decades. Only rarely was it ever commented upon in any newspapers and that was clearly the way Linfield liked it. So when, in September 1979, the *Irish News* ran an excellently-researched and well-argued condemnation of the sectarianism at Windsor Park, the Linfield management committee went mad. They denounced the story as rubbish but they knew, like everyone else, that it was one hundred per cent accurate. Linfield's policy was a disgrace. However, to highlight the issue was viewed as treason by Windsor Park. The article made them look bigoted and foolish. Secretary, Derek Brooks, was quoted as saying that he "was not under the impression that Linfield Football Club was associated with having a sectarian or largely loyalist following." Pardon me? The club chairman, former Ireland cricket captain, Dr Larry Warke refused to co-operate with the *Irish News*. "I don't want to discuss Linfield with the press," he said. "I am sickened by all the fuss created by the media." Apparently, Linfield believed themselves bigger than the problem and, if they just ignored it, it would pack itself up and go away. The ostriches were in danger of being ostracised. I raised the subject at an after-match soiree and a prominent Linfield official told me, "There'll never be a

Catholic in a Linfield shirt in my time here." He was both right and wrong – right in that he would never see the day because he died a few years later; wrong in that Linfield were eventually forced to enter the real world of religious equality.

The pressure had really started to build in the late 1980s when the unspeakable words, "soccer sectarianism", were first used by Father Sean McManus of the Irish National Caucus, in America no less. He turned the screws on Linfield, repeatedly highlighting the sectarian policy at Windsor Park and calling on organisations like Coca Cola to sever their financial ties with the club. Father McManus also urged the government to withdraw funds from Linfield.

Something had to give, though not immediately. Linfield tried to talk their way out of their corner by issuing an unconvincing statement, rejecting claims that they were a bigoted club. The statement denied that Linfield operated a "Protestants only" policy, pointing out it had played seventy Catholics down the years. It didn't, however, acknowledge the absence of Catholics in the side for decades. When manager Eric Bowyer, a Mormon, was quoted as saying, "It would be difficult to envisage the circumstances whereby any local Catholics would even consider joining the Blues", the prospects of an end to the de facto ban on Catholics seemed as remote as ever. Then, Linfield *did* sign a Catholic, almost by accident.

The club recruited a midfield player from Senegal, Tony Coly, who had already received racist abuse from rival fans because of the colour of his skin. A Sunday newspaper really put the cat among the Protestant pigeons when they carried a story revealing that Coly was also a Roman Catholic, thus implying that Linfield hadn't realised his religion when they signed him. Contrary to what Roy Keane said in his autobiography, the club continued to play Coly. Most supporters, in their peculiarly twisted logic, didn't really view Tony as a Catholic because he was African, although one supporter I knew wouldn't go to Linfield matches if Coly was in the starting line-up, and he would actually up and leave the ground if Coly came on as a substitute!

Meanwhile the arguments for Linfield maintaining their religious apartheid were weakening and I sensed the supporters were also mellowing. At one function, organised by a Linfield supporters' club, I broached the subject during my after-dinner speech, saying that I thought it time for Linfield to wise up and welcome more Catholics into their ranks. I expected to be greeted by silence or worse; instead the audience responded with a round of applause. It was clear the climate was changing and, in 1992, Linfield signed their first locally born Catholic in over forty years. Chris Cullen from Downpatrick joined them from Cliftonville and his debut, as a substitute, was marked by a few jeers and considerably more cheers. In one cup game at the Oval, a fan draped a "Fuck off, Chris" banner over the railings but it was hastily removed by a steward.

Later that year, another signing by Linfield's new manager, Trevor Anderson, put the final nail in the coffin of sectarianism at Windsor. Anderson brought former Derry City player Dessie Gorman to Windsor Park. A Catholic from Dundalk, Dessie, in his very first game, won over the most rabid of Linfield fans with his lightning pace and ability to score goals. The supporters dubbed him the "Dundalk Hawk" while Linfield officials banned him from doing press interviews, fearing that someone would ask him about his religion. I kid you not!

A succession of other Catholic signings, many of them from the Republic of Ireland, helped break down the barriers and before too long Linfield were signing young Catholics from west Belfast, something which would have been unimaginable a couple of years earlier. The old guard was changing, leaving some of the fans behind. The club's support remained exclusively Protestant and I had to laugh when I went to Cyprus to cover one of Linfield's European games for UTV. Over a late-night drink, I let slip to a couple of fans that a Linfield player had asked me if I could find out a few GAA results from UTV. The fans wouldn't believe me – they couldn't understand a Linfield player having any interest in Gaelic football. I argued that he probably played Gaelic games at school. These kinds of facts were never included in articles about Linfield's Catholic players. The supporters simply wouldn't let go of their old notions and I decided against telling them about a couple of Linfield players, of the Protestant persuasion, who used to go to Clones in County Monaghan, to watch Gaelic football finals.

However, those Linfield supporters were nothing compared to other nutters I encountered on my soccer travels. The worst incident was in a Glasgow hotel, where I was drinking with friends after a European match. Without warning, a crowd of men to our right suddenly rushed a crowd of men to our left. The ones who didn't get away were beaten to a pulp. There was blood everywhere and the guys who fled were chased through the hotel complex. Anyone still standing got a beating, including Scottish folk unlucky enough to have chosen that hotel for their post-match pint. Our crowd stayed well out of it and sat rooted to the spot, watching in horror. Afterwards, when the dust had settled, one of the protagonists came over to our table and said, "Sorry about that, Ivan. Sorry you had to see that." If the violence hadn't been so disgusting, I would have been tempted to laugh at this man's concern for my sensibilities. Instead I asked him what it was all about. With a straight face, he replied, "Them bastards insulted the Shankill. They're a shower of shite from Coleraine and they were saying things about the Shankill. We showed them that the one thing you can't do is to bad-mouth the Shankill."

Later that night, after the Shankill contingent had left, the Coleraine lads returned to the bar, nursing their wounds. What, I wondered, had they done to warrant their beatings? They said they had been making a joke about Belfast in general, nothing more, nothing less. It reminded me of a riot which had started as Linfield fans were on the boat to England for a European game against Manchester City in the early 70s. Linfield fans from the east and the west of the city had been bantering each other all night in the bar, but when the crowd from the east sang a song about the nationalist politician Gerry Fitt being the other lot's MP, the tables went up in the air and war broke out.

As usual I took the sensible path – out of the bar. I wasn't made for football hooliganism for the very good reason that, as well as being a pacifist, I am also an out-and-out coward. Just call me chicken, yellow belly, wimp. Any one of them will do very nicely, thank you. The nearest I ever came to a personal dust-up was at Coleraine in the 60s when a bloke was arrested at a Linfield match for punching me on the chin. I was only about twelve and I have to confess all these years later that it was actually my fault. Norman and I were standing at the fence at the Showgrounds when Coleraine, who were losing 4-1, staged a remarkable revival, hitting three goals in quick succession to equalise. After the last goal flashed in, a Coleraine fan in front of me waved his scarf in my face. Fuming, I shouted, "Up your hole", and he responded, quite properly, by whacking me on the gub, sending me spinning backwards. As I reeled around, I saw three policemen running towards myself and Norman, who was preparing to deck my assailant. I grabbed him and turned on the waterworks, blubbering to the police that the Coleraine fan had hit me without provocation. The guy tried to explain what I had said but I countered through my tears, "No, mister. I said it was a good goal." At which point the police marched the innocent Coleraine supporter off to the local barracks.

Normally, however, it was Linfield fans that ended up behind bars. Some of the violence in the 60s and 70s was horrific, with the worst of the trouble reserved for games against Belfast rivals, Glentoran. Matches against Derry City at the Brandywell weren't exactly Sunday School outings either. I remember them as draughty affairs. On the journey back from the ground to the railway station, the Derry folk would stone the windows on the buses, while on the trains the Linfield louts would do it themselves, wrecking the windows with their boots. I recall one surprisingly polite hooligan excusing himself as he pushed past our rather sedate bunch to get at a window, which he promptly kicked out before thanking us as he walked out again.

The violence at a European game against Dundalk at Oriel Park in 1979 was the most sickening I have ever experienced, though it certainly wasn't all one-way traffic from Linfield supporters. The game probably should never have been played as it was just days after the IRA had killed Lord Mountbatten at Mullaghmore and eighteen soldiers at Warrenpoint. The tension was heavy in the air and it didn't take long for the inevitable trouble to kick off. The Gardaí baton-charged Linfield fans out of the ground and onto their buses, but the trouble didn't stop there. The buses were ambushed on their way through Dundalk after the game and I had to dive to the floor of my bus to avoid broken glass from the shattered windows. As I lay there, the bloke beside me was happily unwrapping the cling-film around his sandwiches. I silently prayed for survival amidst the onslaught and he offered me a sarnie. I gave him a withering look from under my coat but he persisted, non-plussed, saying "They're smoked salmon, you know." What particularly annoyed me about that night was that I was a closet Dundalk fan. I used to travel down to watch the club on a Sunday afternoon. Where else, I reckoned, could you watch two different leagues on successive days, just fifty miles apart?

Of course, the domestic game in Northern Ireland wasn't alone in its problems with sectarianism. Religion and politics have also plagued Northern Ireland's international team. The furore over Celtic player Neil Lennon, and the sectarian abuse and death threats he received a few years back were nothing new. I remember in the 70s interviewing Pat Jennings, the legendary Northern Ireland goalkeeper from Newry and I remarked that the good thing was that he never got any stick from the red-white-and-blue brigade on the Spion Kop at Windsor Park. They all loved him, I said. Pat put me straight, telling me about a small number of so-called fans who called him everything under the sectarian sun.

Of course, none of this ever made it into the match-day programmes that Billy Kennedy and I edited for the Irish Football Association. Our task was to portray the team and the Association in the best possible light, and that's precisely what we tried to do. The highpoints of my "reign" as joint editor of the publication came in 1982 and 1986, when Billy and I produced special booklets to mark Northern Ireland's appearances in the World Cup finals in Spain and Mexico. I loved being part of the Northern Ireland set-up, having complete access to the players and attending World Cup dinners with them. I would remember how in the late 50s and early 60s Norman, Raymond and I would turn up three hours before kick-off at Northern Ireland internationals, with our Mum's packed lunches in hand to claim our spots. We would be pressed up like sardines against the fencing at Windsor Park to watch our idols like Danny Blanchflower, Peter McParland and Harry Gregg play in front of sixty-three thousand screaming fans, and not one sectarian song in their repertoire.

How all that changed. I will never forget going, in 1982, with Joan and baby Emma to Salou in Spain for a holiday. As Joan and

I enjoyed a late-night/early morning Sangria on our balcony, she said she could hear people singing "The Sash" and "The Billy Boys". I thought it was the drink talking as the town had been as quiet as the grave. Then I could hear the songs too and they were getting louder and louder. On investigation, I discovered hundreds of Northern Ireland fans were arriving on buses to make Salou their base camp for the 1982 World Cup Finals. No one in the travel agency had mentioned that little detail to us when we booked our holiday. To be fair to the fans back then, they weren't the worst in the world and I went with some of them to see the first qualifying match against Yugoslavia in Zaragoza. The match was a bore, a complete contrast to the Irish heroics later in the competition when they beat Spain 1-0.

I rarely go to watch Northern Ireland games now. My heart just isn't in it but the modern-day supporters are trying to stamp out the sectarian rubbish of the past. I am no longer involved in writing for the international programme or for Linfield's publications either. A silly row ended my contributions in 1983. I had stumbled across a story that I wrote for the Linfield programme and I knew it could earn me a few pounds from the Sunday newspapers. It concerned a Linfield supporter whose surname was Park and who was going to call his new-born son Windsor. The Sundays wanted to have the story to themselves and they didn't want it to appear in the *Belfast Telegraph* the day before. This meant my Linfield co-editor abandoning, for one week only, his practice of giving an advance copy of the programme to the *Tele*'s sports editor, Malcolm Brodie. But early on the Saturday morning I got a call from a *Telegraph* reporter seeking a contact number for the Park family. I refused to co-operate so he simply rewrote my article and the Sundays rang me to say they were dropping the story. I was fuming and quit the job immediately.

Seven years later I threw myself into an even bigger project. A friend of mine from UTV, Stephen McCoubrey, approached me to help him produce a video about Linfield's history. The two of us had collaborated on another video about Stephen's own junior team, Bangor Amateurs, and I reckoned the Linfield plan would be an ideal follow-up. Getting co-operation from Linfield wasn't a major obstacle thanks to Stephen's father, Billy, being chairman of the club.

I was determined that the video would be an honest examination of Linfield's story, not a rose-tinted glasses propaganda piece. It was essential to cover the thorny issue of sectarianism despite people advising us to steer clear of it altogether. Anyway we pressed ahead and studied the growth of the club from its Protestant working-class roots, a development mirrored in the Catholic community by Belfast Celtic, who left Irish League football after a riot at Windsor Park in 1948. Thankfully, we had the assistance of the doyen of Ulster soccer journalism, Malcolm Brodie, who added to the credibility of the production with his candid observations about the controversial issues throughout the decades.

I was thrilled with the enthusiastic reviews from independent writers, who applauded our "warts and all" treatment of Linfield's story. I was also delighted that Linfield fans, by and large, acknowledged the way that Stephen and I handled the balancing act between misty-eyed nostalgia and hard-edged reality. One of my sweetest moments was when my mother, who had no real interest in soccer, asked me to bring the video round to her so that we could watch it together and she could try to appreciate what had captivated Norman and me for so many years in our youth. She stayed with it throughout the ninety-minute screening!

In recent times, it must be said, my interest in local soccer has cooled. I still follow the action in the papers and on television, but

I rarely attend matches. Critics say the standard of Irish League
soccer has plummeted in recent years, but they have been
knocking the game here for as long as I can remember. My gripe
is with the introduction to the Irish League of small teams with
small support bases like Loughgall and Dungannon Swifts, the
sort of teams I was covering in my junior soccer column in
Portadown thirty years ago. Once you get out of the habit of
going to watch local games, it's nigh on impossible to rekindle it.
In the past, as many as twenty-five guys used to be part of our
"crowd" at Linfield matches. Now, only about four or five of them
still go, week in and week out. I assume the absentees are, like me,
enjoying the virtual non-stop coverage of Premier League football
from England and Scotland on Sky TV and RTE. When it's a
toss-up between struggling out in the rain to Inver Park in Larne
to watch the local team playing Linfield, or snuggling up on the
sofa to watch Manchester United, Arsenal or Chelsea on RTE,
who would you choose?

Of course, I do miss the days of the big-time in Irish League
football when Linfield commanded crowds of fifteen thousand
and more for home games. I miss watching, from under the old
unreserved grandstand, with its "Gallahers Blues" advertisement,
my heroes like Tommy Dickson, Bobby Braithwaite, Hubert Barr
and Bobby Irvine. The latter was the Linfield goalkeeper in the
team who won those seven trophies I drooled over in 1961-62.

When people ask me about my most difficult interview to date,
I don't say Ian Paisley or Maggie Thatcher – I say Bobby Irvine. I
met him at a players' reunion when I was interviewing people for
the Linfield video. As I tried to ask Irvine my first question, the
only thing that came from my dried-up mouth was a squeak. I was
still star-struck thirty years after Irvine had been a star. My
colleague, Stephen McCoubrey, hastily took over the interview.

The only other time I was too overcome to talk to someone was when I was introduced to the American singer-songwriter, John Prine. A friend had called me backstage at a gig in Letterkenny to meet him. Prine was up there with Springsteen, The Band and Neil Young in my hierarchy of idols and he shook me warmly by the hand, waiting for me to say something sensible. But I couldn't get my brain into gear and my lips wouldn't move. Eventually, Siofra moved in to guide me away like a little boy lost. Please God, never let me meet Pele.

CHAPTER 21

A Little Light Relief

I suppose it has been a bruising old journey, reporting on the troubles for so long, never mind just living in the middle of the violence and trying to bring up a family. Thankfully it hasn't all been tragedy and trauma. I don't know why, but I seem to attract some of the maddest eejits and loopers and it has just happened that many of these encounters have taken place against backdrops of great sadness. Now, I am not making fun of people's misery; that is the last thing I would ever dream of doing. These are simply true tales, not tall tales, and I am unlocking them from my memory bank in no particular order.

I was in New York for 9/11, which was about as unfunny a trip as you could ever get. I was waiting in the Bronx for a priest to return to his office and I went to a nearby shop to buy soft drinks for the team and me. On my return, my cameraman Brian said something odd had happened. As I walked by the window of a bar en route to the shop, a man had dashed out to stare at me. Sure enough, the bloke re-emerged and walked past us several times before asking me with an Ulster-American twang, "Are you the big fucker who used to read the news on UTV?" I replied, "I'm

the big fucker who *still* reads the news on UTV." "Well, fuck me,"
he said. "I told my mate in the bar you looked like the big fucker
who used to do the news back home in Ireland. But he said it was
unlikely that that big fucker would be walking past a bar in the
Bronx. So I told him that I was going to find out if you were the
big fucker or not." After we laughed about the smallness of the
world he told me he was from Bellaghy and couldn't wait to tell
the folks back home about meeting the big fucker from UTV.
Naturally, I insisted, I wasn't actually a big fucker at all but a fairly
decent sort. Still, it all goes to prove that no matter where you go
in the world, you're still the big fucker who reads the news on
UTV. The bloke from Bellaghy had to return a few minutes later
to ask me my name!

I was in Boston to make a documentary when Michael Beattie,
my producer and a superb musician, insisted on going to a music
club where he knew the pianist, and where he had played the
harmonica in the past. Every night after work, we went there until
it slowly dawned on me that it was a gay bar. This was confirmed
when the bartender asked Michael what his wife's name was,
meaning *me*. On the last night Michael's pianist pal wasn't in the
club and we were told she was playing at a place called "Chaps"
nearby. The very name should have sounded alarm bells but we
went on regardless, only to find that this wasn't so much a gay bar
as a transvestites' hang-out. Uncomfortable doesn't come close to
describing my mood. I got even hotter under the collar when
Michael disappeared off to join his ivory-tinkler at the piano,
leaving me alone with a six foot five inches, twenty-stone cross-
dresser called Vera, who wanted to tinkle *my* instrument.
Thinking quickly, I explained to Vera that Michael and I were an
item and he was a particularly jealous man who hated me talking
to anyone else. I minced off as best I could to another part of the

bar. Vera came hulking over to apologise and to say how good a musician Michael was. I don't know why I said it, or where the words came from, but I found myself answering, "Yes, I know. He's just brilliant on the mouth organ. I'm very proud of him." Vera skulked away.

I went to a building in north Belfast for a press conference being staged, ostensibly, by the political allies of a paramilitary group. When we arrived, we were told there was a problem with the electricity so my cameraman went away to get a battery light. I strolled upstairs to a room where I found a team of hooded and armed paramilitaries, who were clearly planning to read out a statement to us. Not quite sure of how to make small talk with masked terrorists, I said, "What's up with the electricity? Not paying your bills, eh?" Quick as a flash, one of the balaclavas, with his AK-47 in hand, replied, "Here, big man, do we look like the sort of boys who pay our electricity bills?"

I was being driven hooded through the County Antrim countryside by another terrorist group, bound for another statement-reading stunt. The usual silence was broken by the sound of a match being struck and the smell of cigarette smoke soon wafted around me. The smoker suddenly remembered his manners. "Sorry, would you like a cigarette?" he asked. I replied, "I'm wearing a flippin' hood. How can I smoke a fag?" to which he mumbled agreeably, "Good thinking, big man!"

The Press Association phoned UTV one day to read over a news story about Haim Hertzog becoming the new President of Israel, and to reveal he had been born in Belfast. On seeing the story, I lamented to the copy-taker that it didn't say if he was a Protestant or a Catholic. The copy-taker went off on one, saying it was typical of journalists to be more interested in the man's religion than his achievement. When I realised she hadn't got my joke I asked her to ring the PA back for more information. I invented a few paragraphs about Hertzog having been a Linfield supporter and a member of the Rising Sons of Tel Aviv Loyal Orange Lodge Number 404 in the Cavehill area of Belfast, and about his love of walking on the Twelfth, holding the banner string. An English colleague then read my nonsense to the copy-taker from another room. Word quickly got around UTV and the newsroom was packed as the copy-taker took down the fiction. She still hadn't wised up to the fact that Hertzog was Jewish and when she finished typing the story, she put down her headphones, stood up and punched the air, shouting, "He's a Prod!"

The *Belfast Telegraph* thought it would be a great idea to photograph me – all six foot three inches of me – recreating an interview I had filmed for UTV, with the little guys from the *Snow White and the Seven Dwarfs* pantomime at the Grand Opera House in Belfast. The photographer set up a snap of me and one of the dwarfs, who came up to just above my knees. I stood moaning and groaning about my embarrassment at being pictured in the middle of a busy Glengall Street, where passers-by were taking the Mickey out of me. My companion looked up at me and shouted, in all sincerity, "Look Ivan, don't be so self-conscious about your height."

I lost my footing on steps at Glengormley where I was covering a bomb alert. As I lay screaming on the ground with a broken ankle, I looked up to see my camerman filming me. "Help me," I yelled at him. "My ankle is swelling up and I can't get my shoe off." He continued rolling until I swore at him to stop. "Why the hell didn't you help me?" I asked him. He replied, "I thought you had been shot and I reckoned the news-desk would have been furious with me if I hadn't got the pictures." Great twit that I am, I was to break the same ankle fifteen years later stepping off a stage during rehearsals for a play in west Belfast. And no, the cameraman didn't keep recording.

I was in the Republic working for ITN and my crew and I were sent south from Dublin to get pictures of an Irish army convoy coming north to the capital, carrying weaponry from an IRA gunship that was captured off the Cork coast. As we travelled south, we passed the convoy going in the opposite direction on a dual carriageway and it was a couple of miles before we could turn around. Going north again, we just couldn't find the convoy. When we reached the convoy's final destination, Garda Headquarters in the Phoenix Park, a guard on the gate said it wasn't due for another hour. We were sure we hadn't passed it on what was the only route to Dublin, so where the hell was it? Had the Provos ambushed it to retrieve their guns? The guard put us out of our misery. "Ach, the soldiers stopped for a cup of tea at the Curragh Army Camp." It was probably the only time in history that one of the world's biggest arms convoys had ever stopped for a brew!

I was covering a loyalist protest in Portadown and not for the first time I was confronted by a demented demonstrator who was unhappy at the way her cause was being reported, especially by me. She ranted on and on, before coming out with the killer line, "I knew your mother, you know. I know what you are, so why don't you give us a good Protestant report tonight? Why don't you stop being so bloody impartial?" It was a good thirty minutes before I realised her insult had actually been a back-handed compliment.

I was taking part in a charity quiz, representing Downtown Radio against the Beeb and UTV. The result hinged on the last question put to a colleague, who was asked to identify a singer on a tape which was playing. He didn't appear to have a clue so I whispered, "Connie Francis." I knew it was her. The more my team-mate pondered, the more I repeated the answer in his ear. Finally he answered, "Shirley Bassey", and we lost. "I told you it was Connie Francis," I said to him later. "Didn't you hear me?" He replied, "I heard you alright. I just didn't want to cheat."

I was at a party in Newry with Siofra, who used to be a member of the Newpoint amateur drama group in the town. Some of her former colleagues were discussing their next youth production and I overheard them saying there were at least six Mexicans in the cast. Thinking this would make a fantastic story, I excitedly approached one of the Newpoint officials for more details. "Oh, the Mexicans? No, they're from Dundalk," she said. I was mystified. "So, why do you call them Mexicans?" I asked. And she replied, "It's because of that song, 'South of the Border, down Mexico way…'"

Emma unwittingly came up with the ideal description of public figures here. As we drove through east Belfast, we passed the Rev Ian Paisley in a car. I asked Emma, who was only about seven at the time, if she knew who he was and what he did. Mixing up the words, politician and representative, she said, "He's a repetition, isn't he?" Out of the mouths of babes.

I was with Siofra on a weekend break to Amsterdam where, naturally, we had a wee peek at the red light district. As we stood outside a sex shop, marvelling at the weird and wonderful things on display in the window, a man walking past said, "Ivan Little,

UTV, more than lively in Amsterdam."

A prisoner who escaped custody from Downpatrick courthouse in May 2003 told friends weeks earlier that he was going to do it. The *Andersonstown News* reported that Ian Carlin said his claim to fame was "going to be scaling the perimeter of a court just as Ivan Little from UTV is outside doing a report about me!"

Gerry Anderson's sidekick on the BBC, Sean Coyle, mimicked my voice for days on end on their morning programme. In a hotel in Derry, as I headed for bed after a charity function, a crowd of people shouted at me to do my UTV sign-off, and so I did. But one of them said, "You're not as good at it as Sean Coyle." How, in God's name, I wondered, could anyone be better at me than *me?*

A social worker friend of mine stopped his minibus near a hotel where I was staying in County Donegal, and told me the kids in the back were all joyriders on a "bit of a break". My concerns weren't exactly eased by his relating how an earlier trip had been abandoned after the joyriders set fire, in the middle of the night, to a disused caravan close to where they had been camping. The riot act was read to the miscreants and they were told to pack for home. "But that's not fair," said a plaintiff voice. "We're hoods. That's what hoods do."

After I had gained a bit of confidence in delivering after-dinner speeches, I came off the stage in a County Down hotel and headed straight for a pressing engagement in the cubicle of a loo. There I listened to one of the guests outside at the urinals rip my speech apart. He said he had heard all the jokes before, which was surprising because they weren't jokes but rather personal anecdotes. I couldn't resist walking out of the cubicle to say "hello" to my critic who nearly wet himself, but not with laughter!

I completely wrecked a stock-car during a "celebrity" race at Dunmore Stadium in Belfast. I was going too fast into a corner and lost control, smashing into a safety barrier. The car, a glorified banger of a clapped-out Ford, fell apart while my bruised pride was my only injury. As I left the stadium, a man came running up to me and shook my hand. "Thanks very much for the entertainment," he gushed. I replied, "But I was the one who crashed and wrecked the car." My grateful admirer said, "I know. That's what I meant. Thanks for the entertainment."

I once scared the living daylights out of the RUC man who was guarding the force's headquarters at Knock. I had been with other reporters, attending one of a regular series of piss-ups with senior officers and, not for the first time, ended up blitzed, especially as the result of an after-hours visit to a detective's office for a taste of his poteen. The next thing I remember is waking up in the toilets at around half past six in the morning. I couldn't find another living soul, so I stumbled down to the security post at the entrance, where a terrified cop nearly had a coronary. "Who the fuck are you?" he shouted. When I explained, he said, "But the last ones left the party four hours ago. How did no one find you?" Good question, I thought, especially as we were talking about one of the most supposedly secure buildings in the world!

I was shooting a short film called *Jumpers* in the centre of Belfast. I was playing the part of a reporter, covering a man who was threatening to kill himself. On a ledge above me was the actor who was preparing "to jump". A sister of a UTV colleague saw the man and the cameras but she didn't see me. She promptly rang our news desk to tip them off that an unfortunate man might soon be plunging to his death. A crew was mobilised and someone rang to see if I could check out the story. I told them I was on a day off, playing the part of a reporter who was covering the make-believe suicide threat, which they thought was a genuine suicide threat and which they wanted this real-life reporter to cover. Yes, it was a bit confusing for me too!

I was preparing a special report on a trial which centred on a murder in the picturesque coastal town of Cushendall in County Antrim. I asked a freelance cameraman to get me shots of specific locations, including the town's Northern Bank, which had been robbed by the same people who were involved in the killing. As I edited my package, I couldn't find the Northern Bank pictures, so I called the cameraman who insisted he had filmed it. He came into UTV to show me where they were and proudly pointed to a beautiful scenic shot of the sea. "There, that's the northern bank of Cushendall, isn't it?" he asked.

And finally, an English colleague in UTV was mystified by an interviewee who had been telling her about a near-miss which her family experienced during a gun battle in Belfast's Turf Lodge estate between the IRA and the army. The woman described how the bullets went everywhere, smashing through windows and embedding themselves in walls and doors – and one even hit the cat. "Was it hurt?" asked my colleague. "Was what hurt?" replied the woman. "The cat," said my colleague. "Was your cat injured?" The incredulous woman replied, "No, not the cat. The *cat* where the baby sleeps…"

Epilogue

Hand on heart, I can honestly say that I love what I do, and what I have done for all of my working life. I can't think of another job where every day is a different day, a day to be enjoyed, not endured. I admit that the boring days can be dreary, dull-as-dishwater yawns but I get a buzz out of waking up in the morning, not knowing what the next eight or nine hours have in store. There can't have been many more adrenalin-rush places to work in the past thirty years than Northern Ireland. I hate hearing people trot out the same old arguments about journalists here being vultures, preying on the vulnerable victims of violence and taking pleasure in other people's misery. That – especially in relation to the journalists who live here – is bull, complete bull. This is my home and home to countless reporters who, like me, could have left to live and work somewhere else. So the problems have been as much our problems as anyone else's.

It hasn't all been bad, and I have been fortunate that UTV give me the freedom to cover all aspects of life here in Northern Ireland as well as the troubles. Down the years I have done my level best to report fairly and objectively, although sometimes it proved almost impossible to keep a balance. A story like the Holy Cross school dispute, where children were caught up in the middle of a sectarian battle of wills, would have taxed the objectivity of Solomon. As I reported, on that first morning the children went to school amid the protests, you could almost taste the hatred in the air, and when I witnessed, two days later, those children running away in terror after a bomb was thrown at them, I felt like packing up and getting out of this place.

Generally though, it has been rewarding for me to feel that I have been accepted in both communities here. I have been honoured, for the last six or seven years, to host the Aisling awards on behalf of the *Andersonstown News*, an unashamedly nationalist newspaper based in west Belfast. The awards are handed over in recognition of outstanding achievements in the world of the arts, sport, business, community leadership and the like. Most of the gongs, though not all of them, have gone to nationalists but the awards *are* reflective of the confidence and vitality of the west of the city. As an east Belfastman, I am sometimes envious of the way the west of the city has blossomed with self-belief and self-assurance. The east is starting to assert itself but there's a long way to go. The Aislings started small – in a pub on the Falls Road – and they have since grown to become a glittering black-tie affair in the Europa Hotel. The organiser, Máirtín Ó Muilleoir, a former Sinn Féin councillor and now boss of the *Andersonstown News* group, has been a dynamo in attracting big names to be guests of honour.

The most emotional Aisling night was two months after 9/11. The organisers invited two NYC firefighters, Gerard O'Hara and Paul McMenamy, to Belfast to accept an award on behalf of their colleagues. They asked me to pay tribute to the firefighters' courage, which wasn't difficult given my experiences in New York after the Twin Towers tragedy.

Another amazing Aisling moment was the night I introduced American Civil Rights campaigner, the Rev Jesse Jackson, in 2004. The hundreds of guests were in awe at sharing the room with him, and I was standing right beside him! Calling him to the stage was an experience I will never forget. At the end of the evening, Jackson left me with a shake of the hand and a booming, "You're the man, big man."

Another regular date on my calendar is the annual Féile an Phobail in west Belfast. The festival was started eighteen years ago as a diversion to the riots that marked the anniversary of internment every year. I host an event on a Saturday morning called *My Kind of People*, which is based on the old Michael Barrymore TV show. I introduce youngsters to strutt their stuff on a stage set up in the Westwood Shopping Centre; singers, dancers, musicians, we get the lot. Gerry Adams, one of the driving forces behind the Féile, usually puts in an appearance, not to sing or dance but to watch from the sidelines. Like Ian Paisley, I get on well with Gerry Adams on a personal level. What I think of Paisley's politics or Adams's politics is another thing entirely, but I like to think I have a healthy rapport with both of them.

Like most of my UTV colleagues, I receive many invitations to functions right across the province. I have opened festivals and church fêtes, judged line-dancing competitions and dog shows, hosted charity concerts, taken part in fund-raisers for good causes, handed over and received cheques for a host of worthy people. In recent times, I have also been asked to take part in functions to collect cash for victims of the tsunami and to relay my experiences of my time in Thailand. I have chaired conferences, the most harrowing of which was in north Belfast, on the highly-charged topic of suicides among young people. What made the task even harder for me on a personal level was the revelation from a woman in the audience that her son, who had taken his own life, had been a youth drama friend of Emma's. I had heard the teenager's name at the time of his death but hadn't made the connection.

The plight of people who lost loved ones during the troubles has also figured heavily in my work as a journalist, whether it's the families of police officers and soldiers who died at the hands of republicans, or relatives of nationalists who were killed by members of the security forces. I have followed the campaigns about two murders particularly closely – the UFF killing of solicitor Pat Finucane in 1989 and the INLA shooting of Billy Wright in 1997. The two groups of campaigners could scarcely be more different but they share the common belief that there was state collusion in the murders. I have come to know and admire Pat Finucane's widow, Geraldine, and Billy Wright's father, David, over the years. The zeal with which they have fought for justice is quite remarkable but it's anyone's guess as to whether they will ever hear the truth.

I have also had uncomfortably close relationships with the people who have been responsible for many murders and there have been times when I have questioned my role as a conduit for terrorist statements. I certainly don't condone or approve of what the paramilitaries have done but I have always tried to act responsibly, trying to expose hypocrisy where there is hypocrisy and lies where there are lies. I have always been wary of using the statements if, by naming people, we would have placed them in even greater danger. The terrorists always knew that I was legally bound to talk to the police after they issued me with their statements and I have frequently been interviewed by detectives, who obviously hoped I could or would identify the people behind the statements. Sometimes I have been given background briefings on behalf of terrorist groups and I haven't given police the names of my contacts on the well-established principle that journalists don't reveal their sources. As far as the paramilitaries are concerned, I deliberately take little notice of my surroundings because I don't really want to know where I am. Get in, get the job done and get out, that's my maxim.

It is not always as easy as it sounds. In July 1997, I received another one of those phone calls telling me to go to a location where the caller said that "Something interesting might just happen." I was instructed to go to a street in the Woodvale area of Belfast to wait and watch. Shortly after I arrived, with a cameraman, six masked and armed men ran out of an alleyway, carrying two AK-47 rifles, an Uzi submachine gun, an SA80 rifle and a Heckler and Koch rifle. They brazenly walked up and down the street for about five or six minutes before disappearing. I was told they were from the UVF and the UDA and were defending their streets against nationalist attacks, a rare display of unity from rival terrorists who were known more for their feuding than their friendship. What shocked me about this show of strength was the nonchalance with which the terrorists mounted it. They seemed cock-sure that no police or army patrols would come into the area to catch them in the act. Of course, if the security forces had arrived, I would have been hauled off to court as well, although I hadn't known in advance what was going to happen.

Thankfully, the men in the balaclavas haven't been the only people in my journalistic life. Reporting on the colourful characters that pop up everywhere in Northern Ireland has helped me keep sane during the craziness of the troubles. As I've mentioned, I have been fortunate that UTV have allowed me to cover so many different types of stories. Some broadcasting bosses insist that reporters stay in one particular box. I have enough confidence in my ability to report with equal assurance on hard or soft news but you still need backing from above and that has never been a problem in UTV. This probably explains why it has been the breeding ground for so many excellent broadcasters, like Gordon Burns, Gloria Hunniford, Eamonn Holmes and latterly Johnny Irvine of ITN.

People occasionally ask me if I am jealous of people like

Eamonn and Johnny and the answer is no. I am proud of and take delight in their achievements. I still get a buzz, recalling how former colleagues in the *Belfast Telegraph*, like Denis Murray and Gavin Esler, used to come to me for advice with their stories. I was only a couple of years older than them, but had been longer in the game. Besides, I never wanted to cross the water to work, probably owing to the difficulties in my private life more than anything else. Still, staying here has enabled me to follow my parallel dream of acting, something I would definitely not have been able to do in England.

With regard to the troubles, however, one murder has lived in my memory with crystal clarity and, as I ruminated about whether or not to include it in these pages, the strangest thing happened. During the spring of 2005, I was talking to another veteran reporter of the troubles in a courthouse in Dungannon. Graham Bardgett worked for the *Belfast Telegraph* before going on to the *Daily Mail* and the BBC. After a spell in England, he has recently returned to work for the *Daily Mirror* and, as we talked about our memories of the violence here, he told me that one killing had also stayed with him. Incredibly, he singled out the very murder that has haunted me.

It was the murder in October 1981 of Catholic father-of-three, Bobby Ewing, in his home on the Deerpark Road in north Belfast. What made me remember him? Well, it wasn't his name even though it was also the name of a main character in the hugely popular TV series, *Dallas*. It wasn't even the fact that he had been shot as he watched a TV report of mine about another funeral. And it wasn't the fact that his home was on one of the newspaper delivery routes operated by my father when he owned a shop at Cliftonville Circus. No, what imprinted the murder in my mind was the way his wife spoke so graphically, while in a state of complete disbelief, about the way he was killed.

Mrs Ewing described to me how a gunman burst into the living room: "I just saw the gun, I heard the bang and I smelled the gunpowder, and I saw Bobby's eye just shoot out of his head. I don't think he knew he had been hit." Mrs Ewing believed her husband had been shot by his loyalist killers because he was a Catholic. The police confirmed his being a totally innocent random victim who didn't belong to any organisations. As for the UFF gunmen, Mrs Ewing said, "I just hope they burn in Hell."

Like me, Graham had a flawless recollection of what Mrs Ewing said. What I had not remembered was Graham in the living room as I conducted the interview with her, taking notes of the conversation. Just why Mr Ewing's killing should have had such an impact on Graham and myself is a mystery, for there have, tragically, been thousands of victims like Bobby Ewing. Hopefully, however, there won't be thousands more.

As for the future, my scepticism about the prospects for peace is still as ingrained as ever. Yet the fact that there has been a peace of sorts for more than a decade can't be ignored, not even by an old cynic like me. The IRA's statement in the summer of 2005, effectively signalling an end to their thirty year campaign, is quite clearly a start, but even if they were to vanish and take the loyalist paramilitaries with them I can't see the cancer of sectarianism following them. The hatred here is still depressingly tangible. One of the most disheartening things I have heard in years is that some children from Northern Ireland, who go on cross-community holidays, apparently use knowledge acquired on these excursions about their peers from the other side to single these individuals out for sectarian attacks back home.

The appetite for a return to the bad old, mad old days of violence does appear to have waned, for this generation at least. It's hard to imagine us going back to the blackest days in the 70s when a story I wrote about ten deaths over a single weekend didn't even make the front page of the *Belfast Telegraph*. It had been overtaken by an even greater, and fresher, headline-grabbing atrocity.

It's eight years since I first heard the words "The war is over" from a Provo taxi driver who was transporting me to a late-night drinking session in Derry. He wanted to know how I felt about the peace process and informed me that he had done time for "something" in the 70s. In response to my declaration that I didn't feel the restored IRA ceasefire of 1995 would last he said, "It's gone, big man. The only thing is it could be years before anyone says officially that it's over, if they ever do." I reckon now that he was giving me the inside track but I only wish he had told me when exactly the peace would begin.

If *The History of the Troubles* is ever revived in years to come, I would love to see the ending of the play, which is currently embedded in the uncertain limbo of 2005, rewritten. If my character in the play, Gerry Courtney, could truly declare that the troubles really are history, that would definitely be phenomenal.